Linen and Cotton

Classic Sewing Techniques for Great Results

Susan Khalje

The Taunton Press

Cover photos: Jack Deutsch
Author photo: June Chaplin

Taunton
BOOKS & VIDEOS
for fellow enthusiasts

Printed in the United States of America
10 9 8 7 6 5 4 3 2

The Taunton Press, 63 South Main Street
PO Box 5506
Newtown, CT 06470-5506
e-mail: tp@taunton.com

Distributed by Publishers Group West

Library of Congress Cataloging-in Publication Data

Khalje, Susan.
    Linen and cotton : classic sewing techniques for great results /
Susan Khalje.
        p.   cm.
    Includes index.
    ISBN 1-56158-250-6
    1. Dressmaking.   2. Tailoring (Women's).   3. Cotton fabrics.
4. Linen.   I. Title.
TT557.K43   1999   98-33436
646.4 — dc21   CIP

Acknowledgments

My thanks to the following for their generosity:

Karen Anderson

Colleen Jones

Dolores Luckow

Sarah Veblen

Marion Whitlock

Handler Textiles

Masters of Linen/Confédération Européene du Lin et du Chanvre

And to my editors, Jolynn Gower, Sarah Coe, Ruth Dobsevage, and Peter Chapman, my thanks for your help, your encouragement, your enthusiasm, and your support.

For information about the Couture Sewing School, write to Susan Khalje at PO Box 51, Long Green, MD 21092.

Contents

Introduction

My first sewing project was made out of cotton, and I am willing to bet that yours was too. I made a purple gingham pillow cover in Home Economics class. I loved it and can still remember slip-stitching it closed (I thought the slip-stitch was the cleverest thing I'd ever seen). Ever since that first experience I have loved the straightforward charms of cotton and its close friend, linen.

With all of today's emphasis on the newest, the latest, the most high-tech, it's refreshing to rediscover the classics: linen and cotton. But classic doesn't have to mean boring. I visited a fine fabric store the other day and was amazed by the huge variety of cottons and linens that I found—from playful to quietly elegant to vibrant to sophisticated. It was truly inspiring.

Linens and cottons are easy to find, easy to work with, and easy to wear and maintain. They are reasonably priced and available in an astonishing range of weights and weaves: from the softest cotton lawns, voiles, and handkerchief linens to the sheerest dotted Swiss, batistes, and organzas to the crispest piqués, chintzes, ginghams, and polished cottons to the most elegant European prints and matelassés to delicately intricate eyelets, laces, and embroideries to the firmest ottomans, failles, twills, and ducks to the sturdiest canvases and heavy-weight linens. Despite their enormous variety, what these fabrics do have in common is a straightforward ease of handling, along with predictable behavior and uncomplicated wear and care. Like the best of friends, linen and cotton fabrics are cooperative and dependable, and seldom difficult.

A garment may begin with design or fabric, but its ultimate success depends upon the compatibility of the two. In turn, that rests largely with the sewer's familiarity with the fabric. What does it love to do? What does it hate to do? What does it do well? What does it resist doing? Answer these questions and you'll be able to make the most of your fabric.

As this is a fiber-oriented book (as opposed to a garment-oriented book), it's useful to have at least a basic acquaintance with fibers, processing, weaves, dyeing techniques, and finishes. Although similar in many ways, linen and cotton react differently to processing and surface treatments. What they have in common is that they're grown, harvested, processed, woven, dyed, and treated—usually, but not always, in that order. Not only is the processing of these fibers a fascinating subject in itself, a familiarity with it will broaden your knowledge and appreciation of them, and make you better able to use them well.

Included in this book are a number of sample garments, which cover a range of styles, fabrications, and techniques. The garments range from the elegant to the casual, from styles with careful shaping to those that are soft and flowing. You'll see the broad range of cottons and linens put to their best use, with a variety of applications for seams, seam finishes, pockets, closures, hems, and finishing details.

Linen and cotton fabrics can serve for many occasions. As you get to know them, or get to know them better, you'll discover their individuality and come to appreciate their charms. You'll also learn how to choose and care for cotton and linen before, during, and after construction, so you can use them with confidence from start to finish. I know you'll enjoy choosing them, working with them, and wearing them.

1

Linen and Cotton Fabrics

Linen and cotton are delightful fabrics to sew—there's little they can't do and little they won't do. They're a dressmaker's dream: They do exactly what they're told, and they show off details beautifully. Just as rewarding as the finished product is the fun of sewing with linen and cotton. I can think of few other fabrics to rival cotton and linen's charms—they're honest, straightforward, and well-behaved fabrics, with only pleasant surprises in store for you.

LINEN

If, as the current slogan goes, cotton is "the fabric of our lives," then linen is surely the fabric of our history. It's hard to imagine that the same fiber that the Phoenicians made into sails for their ships was also used to create the finest lace in 16th-century Europe, or that the ancient Egyptians were able to produce linen fabric—manually—of a fineness unequaled today. Linen comes from the flax plant, whose Latin name translates to "most useful linen." As you'll see, no name could be more appropriate.

In continuous use for 10,000 years, linen is the oldest fiber known to man. It's even included in the mythology of a number of cultures, including that of the Egyptians, who credited the goddess Isis with the gift of linen, and the northern Europeans, who believed that the Teutonic earth-goddess Hilda taught mankind how to grow flax and process linen. Linen has been found among the remains of the Swiss lake dwellers of Neolithic times. Its use later spread as the Phoenicians, the great traders of the ancient world, sold it and bartered it. By the 10th century, linen weaving was the national industry of Flanders, and it continued to grow in popularity throughout Europe.

It was fine linen threads that were used to make the legendary European laces in the 16th century, although the conditions under which they were produced were appalling. Apart from the painstakingly slow rate of production itself, lacemakers worked in damp basements (to keep the fibers from drying out) with limited light. Often the light from a single candle was all that was allowed, lest the lace be discolored

by the candle soot. Perhaps it was a blessing that lace declined in popularity at the time of the French Revolution and that the Industrial Revolution introduced lace-making machines.

Linen was ideally suited to the temperate European climate. While cotton required heat to grow (hence its popularity in India and the American South), linen adapted well to the growing conditions in Europe. Russia is the biggest producer of linen today, with Europe's production (centered in France, Belgium, and the Netherlands) second. The linen produced in western Europe is considered to be superior, because it is grown under ideal conditions and manufactured according to strict standards of quality.

Characteristics of linen

If you were to create the perfect fiber, much of what you'd ask for is present in linen. Its unique combination of strength and beauty as well as its legendary comfort are but two of its many attributes. The fact that it's prone to wrinkling seems to be a small price to pay, given its other charms.

Although labor intensive to harvest and produce, linen's remarkable versatility—and its suitability for household, interior, and fashion fabrics—makes it irresistible. Its absorbent properties are legendary; it can absorb up to 20% of its weight before feeling damp. It easily releases its moisture (its core is hollow, and under a microscope, resembles bamboo), making it the coolest fabric to wear. Its smooth fibers with their anti-static properties repel dirt. In fact, the fiber sheds a microscopic layer with every laundering. Not only is soil carried away, but a fresh surface is also exposed.

Linen's fibers do not fray or rub, so neither lint nor static is created. The list of its other qualities is impressive: It is fade resistant, colorfast, softer and stronger when

used, mildew and moth resistant, and non-allergenic. Its durability is unmatched.

Processing

The processing of flax into fiber is ecologically sound. No pesticides are used in its cultivation, and every part of the plant is put to use in some way: By-products include cattle feed, rope, paper, ink, paint, and linseed oil. Sown at the end of March or the beginning of April, flax, with its soft blue flowers, is ready to harvest 100 days later, after the plant has reached its full height of 2 ft. to 3 ft.

Pulled by the roots rather than cut (to maximize the length of the fibers), flax plants are bundled and left in the field. The seeds are removed and are used either for sowing the next year's crops or for producing linseed oil. In a process called retting, during which the bundles of flax are left outdoors or soaked inside in warm water, the plants begin to decompose. As natural enzymes break down the flax, the fibers start to separate from the rest of the plant. If the bundles are retted outside, the fibers are bleached by the sun.

Next comes scutching, which separates the fibers in the stem from the woody matter and bark of the plant. The fibers are rubbed and beaten, and the smaller, coarser, broken fibers (the tow fibers) are separated from the longer fibers. Ultimately, roughly two-thirds of the fibers will be suitable for processing into quality linen, while the remaining one-third, the tow fibers, will be used for coarser fabrics.

The fibers are then combed through a series of progressively finer rollers. The longer, smoother fibers are wound in preparation for spinning. Flax is wet spun, meaning that the fibers pass through a trough of hot water just before they're spun. The water bath softens the natural gum, yielding a higher-quality fiber. Flax fibers are long and smooth, without any crimp, so they must be tightly spun, or they will work apart.

Weaving

While cotton's appeal often comes from vibrant prints, linen's more commonly arises from interesting textures and weaves. Today's sophisticated technology can produce a wide array of weaves, rich in variety and texture, ranging from the rustic effects that we traditionally associate with linen, to the gossamer, and everywhere in between.

Linen is complicated to weave because the fibers lack elasticity, but a number of technical advances have resulted in yarns that are stronger and better suited to today's high-speed looms. New warping techniques produce better tension during weaving and improve linen's elasticity, and some yarns are treated with paraffin (later removed) to soften them for knitted linens.

Linens today are woven into crepes, tweeds, and bouclés. They are sanded and pumiced, and they are blended with other fibers to lessen their penchant for wrinkling and to add bounce. Mother-of-pearl and other iridescent finishes are applied to enhance linen's natural shine and luster, and its inherent fiber strength allows fine open semisheer weaves that still maintain a crisp hand.

Dyeing

There are a number of methods of dyeing linen. It can be yarn dyed, in which the yarn is dyed before weaving, or piece dyed, in which the woven fabric is dyed. Linen is always opened to its full width during dyeing and finishing.

Jigg-dyeing is a method of dyeing in which a roll of fabric is mounted on a type of dyeing machine called a jigg. The fabric is then run through a dye bath and wound up onto a second roll. The process is repeated, with the fabric wound back and forth, until the proper depth of color is achieved.

Union dyeing is a method of dyeing used with fabric that contains fibers with different dyeing affinities. To produce a homogenous color, each fiber will require the use of a number of dyes.

Treatments and finishes

Linen goes through a series of finishing treatments, resulting in fabrics that are more lustrous, softer, and crease resistant than before (see the sidebar below). Given its propensity for wrinkling, crease resis-

LINEN TREATMENTS AND FINISHES

- **Calendering.** The cloth is passed through two or more cylinders. The pressure they create is used to apply surface treatments, embossing among them, to fabric.

- **Friction calendering.** The cloth is passed between heated rollers that rotate at slightly different speeds. The resulting friction makes the fabric lustrous.

- **Softening.** Lubricant chemicals are applied to soften and counteract stiffness.

- **Beetling.** Damp fabric is wound around a metal cylinder and hammered by heavy wooden mallets, flattening the fibers and increasing their luster.

- **Bleaching.** While linen is sometimes bleached through exposure to sun, air, and moisture, chlorine and hydrogen peroxide are usually used to bleach it and other similarly constructed cellulosic fibers.

- **Mercerizing.** A process that immerses material in caustic soda (which is later neutralized in acid), the treatment permanently swells the fibers, increasing their strength and the fibers' affinity for dyes. It also adds dimensional stability, making the fabric less likely to shrink.

- **Starching.** The linen thread is treated with starch, which renders it smoother and tighter, making it easier to weave.

tance has long been a goal of linen manufacturers, so resins are often baked onto fabrics, creating chemical bonds that make the fabric more resistant to wrinkling.

Among the new finishes are enzyme washes, applied to the yarn or the fabric, to give a softer hand and reduce wrinkling. There are also new formaldehyde-free resins, applied for the same reason.

Judging quality

As with all fabrics, price is one indicator of quality. Many European linens are now sold under the Masters of Linen label, which guarantees a high-quality product manufactured under high standards. But beyond those general guidelines, here are some specific things to look for when shopping for linen:

- *The fabric should feel cool and smooth to the touch, unless purposely woven to feel otherwise.*
- *There should be no visible raw plant fibers.*
- *When held up to the light, the dye should be evenly distributed throughout the fabric.*
- *There should be no large knots.*
- *Short surface fibers should have been removed.*
- *The fabric should be lustrous.*
- *Although linen can have a dry feel, it shouldn't feel brittle and stiff.*
- *The weave should be sufficiently firm. Linen is a smooth fiber, without natural crimp; and unless it is tightly woven, the fabric will be inferior, unstable, and disappointing to work with.*
- *If the linen has been folded on the bolt, the crease shouldn't show any deterioration of color. Consider purchasing extra fabric in case the crease turns out to be impossible to remove.*
- *The grain should be straight or able to be straightened. Linen's grain is almost always visible and is an important part of its appeal. Off-grain fabric will not only be difficult to work with but will also spoil the appearance of the finished garment. If the linen has been treated, the grain may be impossible to realign.*

COTTON

Cotton, the most widely used fiber in the world, has a long and fascinating history. Cotton was used in India thousands of years ago and has been traced to ancient Egypt, Greece, Rome, and pre-Columbian America. It was introduced to Europe by Arab traders (the word "cotton" comes from *qutun*, the Arabic name for cotton), and its use there became widespread in the 17th century as trade with India increased. In France, its popularity grew after the French Revolution, as that of silk, associated with the aristocracy, declined. Unlike flax, cotton is a warm-weather crop.

In America, cotton's first commercial use was in Jamestown in 1607. The invention of the cotton gin in 1791 by Eli Whitney, along with advances in England during the Industrial Revolution, had a profound effect on the industry, leading to huge increases in production. Cotton still needed to be harvested by hand, however, so the use of slaves, which had been in decline at the end of the 18th century, eventually quadrupled to match the output needed. Favorable growing conditions in the southern United States, the development of more sophisticated looms, access to water for both transportation and as a source of power in the North, where cotton was processed, all contributed to the industry's growth. By the 1820s, cotton mills were widespread in both the North and the South; and by 1860, the United States was exporting over 2.5 million bales of cotton each year to England and producing two-thirds of the world's supply. Although now rivaled by China, the United States was until recently the world's largest producer of cotton.

Characteristics of cotton

It is cotton's hollow fibers that make it breathe, make it absorbent, and make it comfortable to wear. It resists mildew and moths, dyes beautifully, and can tolerate high temperatures without its fibers being weakened. Its fibers have little elasticity, though, so it does wrinkle easily, and it can be weakened if exposed to sunlight for an extended period.

Shrinkage is also a factor. Although cotton fibers themselves don't shrink, cotton fabrics do. Cotton yarns are woven under tension, and when the fabric is taken off the loom, the threads relax. Subsequent washing and steaming return them to their original size. Although most shrinkage happens during the initial washing, there is sometimes progressive shrinkage, in which the fabric shrinks a little more each time it's washed.

Processing

Most cotton today is picked by machine. Although not as selective as hand-picking, machine picking increases the yield dramatically—nearly 50-fold.

After picking, cotton is ginned. In addition to removing seeds and impurities, ginning begins the process of separating short fibers from longer fibers. The short fibers are used for lint and in the production of rayon, and the seeds are processed into cottonseed oil and fertilizer. The fibers are then carded (to clean them and further make them parallel), drawn (to straighten and strengthen them), and sometimes combed (which further straightens them and removes all shorter fibers). Finally, the fibers are spun into continuous threads and then woven.

Fibers, or staples, range from extra short (less than ¾ in. long) to short (¾ in. to 1 in. long) to medium (1 in. to 1⅛ in. long) to long (1⅛ in. to 1⅜ in. long) to extra long (1⅜ in. to 2½ in. long). Although the majority of cotton raised falls in the middle category, the premium varieties of cotton—Egyptian, Peruvian, Pima, and Sea Island—all fall into the final category.

Weaving

Cotton is available in an enormous variety of weights and weaves. The addition of finishing processes and treatments makes the range practically infinite. See the chart on p. 10 for a listing of the most common weaves.

Dyeing and printing

Cotton is most commonly dyed by two methods: yarn dyeing, in which the yarn is dyed before it is woven, and piece dyeing, in which the fabric is dyed after it is woven. Almost all solid-color fabrics are piece dyed. Printing, which is the application of a pattern after the cloth has been woven, ranges from the simplest hand-blocking to techniques that employ complicated and sophisticated machinery (see the sidebar below).

COTTON PRINTING TECHNIQUES

- **Discharge printing.** Chemicals are applied to an already dyed fabric, bleaching out part of the color. A white pattern on a dyed background results.

- **Resist printing.** In this three-step process, a design is first printed with a dye-resistant paste. The fabric is then piece dyed. Finally, the dye-resistant paste is removed, leaving a white pattern behind.

- **Roller printing.** Fabrics are passed over engraved rollers. The most advanced machines can accommodate up to 16 colors, each of them perfectly registered on the fabric.

- **Screen printing.** A design is blocked on a screen, forming a sort of stencil, then dye is squeezed through the unblocked part of the screen. A different screen is required for each color.

COTTON WEAVES

LIGHTWEIGHT

BATISTE A sheer, smooth, fine plain-weave cotton that has usually been mercerized.

DOTTED SWISS Similar to lawn and decorated with evenly placed dots, which can be woven in or applied with an adhesive.

GAUZE A thin, sheer fabric with an open weave.

LAWN A fine, soft, relatively sheer, plain-weave fabric.

ORGANDY A sheer light-weight fabric with a very crisp hand. It may be starched, or its fibers may be treated to make it perma-nently crisp.

PERCALE A plain-weave lightweight cotton with a firm hand.

VOILE A lightweight sheer fabric whose filling yarns are tightly twisted, giving it a crisp hand.

MEDIUMWEIGHT

BATIK A fabric treated with a resist-dye technique that uses wax as the resisting agent. The technique origi-nated in Bali.

BROADCLOTH Similar to poplin, broadcloth is a plain-weave fabric whose filling yarns are heavier than its warp yarns. It was originally woven on broad looms, hence its name.

CALICO Although calico has come to mean cotton fabrics printed with small, busy pat-terns, it originally referred to hand-blocked fabrics import-ed from Calicut (Calcutta, India) in the 17th century.

CHALLIS A soft, plain-weave fabric, usually printed with flowers.

CHAMBRAY A plain-weave, yarn-dyed fabric in which the warp is colored and the weft, or filling, yarns are white. It is often used for shirts.

CHINTZ Printed or plain fabric that has been treated to give it a temporary or permanent glazed finish. The term originally referred to block-printed fabric from India.

GINGHAM A yarn-dyed, plain-weave fabric that can be woven in two colors (checks) or more (plaid).

MUSLIN A plain-weave fab-ric with a firm hand, woven in a variety of weights. It may be bleached or unbleached.

OTTOMAN A lustrous plain-weave fabric with large, round horizontal ribs.

PLISSÉ A cotton fabric in which part of the cloth has been treated with caustic soda, causing it to shrink. A puckered, or blistered, effect is produced.

POPLIN A durable plain-weave fabric whose warp yarns are finer than its filling yarns, giving it a ribbed appearance.

SEERSUCKER A cotton fab-ric in which the tension of the warp threads has been varied to produce crinkled stripes and taut stripes.

HEAVYWEIGHT

CANVAS Its name often used interchangeably with duck, canvas is a firm, closely woven fabric. Canvas general-ly refers to the heavier weights of the weave.

DENIM A sturdy twill-woven fabric. The warp is generally blue with white filling.

DRILL A densely constructed fabric similar to denim, woven with coarse yarns in a twill (diagonal) weave.

DUCK A very sturdy plain-weave fabric that can range from firm to pliable. Its use is often industrial: sails, awnings, and tents.

TWILL A fabric woven with a twill weave, which is charac-terized by a diagonal rib. Twills are firm, strong, and durable, and often used for menswear.

SPECIALTY WEAVES

BROCADE A fabric woven on a jacquard loom, often with floral designs, which uses a combination of twill, plain, and/or satin weaves to create raised patterns. Filling yarns are sometimes used to add thickness to certain parts of the design, and metallic yarns are often used as well.

CHENILLE Chenille is woven from yarns in which the fibers protrude on all sides from a twisted base yarn. The term comes from the French word for caterpillar.

DAMASK A jacquard-woven fabric, in which the pattern appears to have been embossed. Different weaves are alternated to distinguish the patterns; a design may be in a satin weave, its back-ground may be in a twill weave. True damasks are flat and reversible.

FAILLE A sturdy, flat-ribbed, plain-weave fabric, in which the filling yarns are heavier than the warp yarns.

FLANNEL A soft plain- or twill-weave fabric in which the filling yarns are napped (brushed). Flannel can be napped on one side or both sides.

JACQUARD A figured pat-tern made possible by the development and refinement of the jacquard loom by the Frenchman Jean-Marie Jacquard in 1801. The loom allows very elaborate designs to be woven. Brocade and damask are jacquard fabrics.

MATELASSÉ A fabric in which crepe yarns and ordi-nary yarns are interlaced. In the finishing process, the crepe yarns shrink, giving the fabric its puckered appearance.

PIQUÉ A double cloth in which there are two sets of warp yarns and two sets of filling yarns, produced in a variety of patterns.

Treatments and finishes

A number of treatments and finishes are commonly applied during the processing of cotton (see the sidebar at right). One treatment—beetling—gives cotton the appearance of linen.

Judging quality

Price is often an indicator of superior cotton, but there are many other factors to consider as well:

* *The yarn should be strong and evenly spun, not weak and uneven.*
* *The weave should be sturdy and even. If scraping your fingernail across the fabric distorts the weave, it may be too unstable for your purposes.*
* *Superior cottons are woven from long-staple fibers—they will be more lustrous in appearance and will wear well.*
* *The grain should be consistent. Does it straighten easily or will it be difficult to alter? Certain finishes, such as permanent press, make altering the grain impossible.*
* *Is the color even? Is the fabric dyed well and consistently? Will the dye crock (rub off)? Is there fading along a fold line if the fabric has been stored on a flat bolt? Can the fold line be pressed out, or can you avoid it in your layout?*
* *If the fabric is a stripe or a check, is it woven in or printed? A poorly registered printed stripe or check may be impossible to work with. If the pattern is printed, it should be even and well registered.*
* *Has the fabric been treated with a surface finish? Is the finish permanent? Will the finish be an asset or a liability? Can the surface treatment be scratched away with your fingernail? Often, inferior fabrics are heavily sized, making them appear initially stronger and more durable than they really are.*

COTTON TREATMENTS AND FINISHES

* **Mercerizing.** A process developed in 1844 by an English calico printer, John Mercer. He found that saturating the fibers with caustic soda (later neutralized) causes them to swell permanently, increasing their luster, their strength, and their ability to take dyes.

* **Beetling.** Damp fibers are pounded with heavy mallets as they pass through a machine, a process that flattens out rounded fibers, giving them the appearance of linen.

* **Glazing.** The fabric is treated with starch, wax, paraffin, or synthetic resins, producing a polished surface.

* **Sizing.** Synthetic resins are applied to the yarns to enhance their smoothness, weight, luster, and strength. Sizing is sometimes permanent, sometimes not.

* **Calendering.** An ironing process used to give surface effects to fabrics. The fabric is passed between cylinders, one or more of which may be heated. Embossing and moiré are calendered finishes. Calendering is not always a permanent finish.

* **Permanent press.** Fabric—either yardage or a finished garment—is treated with chemicals, resins, or heat.

BLENDS

A blend is a textile that contains two or more generic (basic) fibers, or sometimes two different types of the same fiber. The advantage of a blend is that certain negative properties of a fiber can be corrected or diminished, by adding another fiber. The components can be melded in the spinning process, or later in the weaving process. The warp and weft might be woven of two different fibers, for example, or of two fibers that react differently to the dyeing process.

Technological advances have led to many successful linen blends, such as linen/silk, linen/viscose, and linen/polyester. Cotton and linen themselves are often blended together, resulting in a fabric with the visual appeal of linen but with some of the softness of cotton. Cotton is often blended with polyester to create an economical fabric that is stronger and less prone to wrinkling than cotton alone. Comfort is affected, though, as polyester doesn't breathe the way cotton does.

There are also three-way blends: Linen/cotton/viscose, linen/viscose/poly, and linen/viscose/lycra are successful combinations. While other fibers are often added to linen, linen itself is often added to other fibers to increase their water absorption and make them more comfortable to wear.

CARING FOR LINEN AND COTTON

Linen and cotton are easy fabrics to care for. Strong fibers to begin with, and even stronger when wet, they can withstand heat, bleach, agitation, machine drying, and the hottest of irons.

Laundering today takes minutes, but that has not always been the case. In 18th-century Europe, household linens were soaked and scrubbed indoors, rinsed outdoors in running water, and spread out to dry in fields. They were sprinkled with water to extend the drying process, which would last for several days. Finally, the linens were folded and then ironed while damp. The bleaching fields of northern Europe were renowned for a seemingly magical combination of sunlight, moonlight, and dew, merging to form a chemical reaction that brilliantly whitened linens.

Today, the steps we use are similar (soaking, scrubbing, rinsing, drying, and ironing), but the soaps have been refined and the time the process takes has been drastically reduced. Linen is straightforward to wash and tends to shed soil easily. The most important part of the process, though, is thorough rinsing. Detergents left in the fabric may cause linen's fibers to oxidize. Over time, this can cause spotting.

Although bleaching is a part of the manufacturing process of linen and cotton, strong bleach is eventually harmful to both fibers. With linen, chlorine bleach is best avoided, as it can degrade the fibers and cause yellowing. Cotton can also be bleached by sunlight, although long-term exposure will cause the fibers to deteriorate and eventually yellow.

It's best to iron linen while damp. Linen can become brittle if allowed to dry out thoroughly, although it will, in time, re-absorb moisture from the air. Linen can withstand the highest of temperatures, but it does have a tendency to glaze. It's best to iron dark linens on the wrong side only. Ornamentation of a dimensional nature should be ironed face down into a thick towel to avoid flattening it out.

When heavy linens are deeply wrinkled, it may be wisest to ask your dry cleaner to press the fabric or the garment. It's inexpensive, and unless you have access to professional equipment, your dry cleaner will be able to do a better job than you can.

Although linen is mildew and moth resistant, it should be stored in a well-ventilated area. With linens that are folded, rearrange the fold lines from time to time. Don't store linen in plastic bags, directly against wood, or in cardboard boxes—paper and wood contain acids that will damage the fabric. Store them instead in acid-free cardboard boxes with acid-free tissue paper.

Removing stains

Before treating any stains, check the fabric for colorfastness. When linen is dyed, the dye often doesn't fully penetrate the fibers. Much of the dye remains on the surface of the fabric and will be rubbed off if the fabric is abraded to remove a stain. The stain may disappear, but so will some of the dye, or anything else—sizing and resins—that has been applied to the fabric.

The sooner spots can be treated, the better. A spot becomes, in time, a stain. The idea of stain removal is to break up the spot and absorb it, as it's released, onto clean, white absorbent material. To this end, place layers of clean cheesecloth or white paper towels under the stain to absorb it. (Normally the stain is worked from the underside, forcing it downward, away from the fabric. The stain has to go somewhere, and you don't want it to be reabsorbed onto the fabric.) Replace the cheesecloth or paper towels as the stain releases. Tamp (hit) the spot to break it up. Avoid the temptation to rub, because rubbing will only abrade the fibers.

Stains are usually oil-based, water-based, or a combination of the two. Use a solvent to treat oil-based stains; adding water will only make it more difficult to remove them. Flush the stain with a solvent, tamp it to break up the stain, then blot it to absorb the solvent. Flush it again with solvent, and feather the edges of the solvent to prevent a ring from forming. Use a detergent to treat water-based stains. Wet the stain, apply the detergent, tamp to break up the stain, and flush with water. Repeat the process, and feather the edges of the wet area to prevent the formation of a ring. If a stain is a combination, start with a solvent, then move on to a detergent.

Stubborn stains can be treated with vinegar, then peroxide (they're both mild bleaches). If bleach is used, follow it with vinegar to neutralize it and keep the fabric from yellowing.

Scorch marks, common when ironing linen and cotton at high temperatures, often result from a build-up of starch or detergent. Treat them with a solution of 1 part hydrogen peroxide to 2 parts water. Let the garment soak, then rinse it thoroughly.

Vintage cotton garments are easy to find but may need some cleaning to restore them to their original beauty.

Caring for vintage garments

Linen and cotton are sturdy fibers, so vintage cotton and linen garments are quite common in clothing and antique shops (see the sidebar on p. 121). To clean these garments, soak them in a pure soap, changing the water as soon as it becomes dirty. Be sure to support the weight of the garment as you rinse it. Careful and thorough rinsing, while tedious, is essential.

A paste of lemon juice and salt will remove mildew, rust, and scorch marks, all of which are common stains on vintage garments. Cotton and linen need to be clean and dry before being stored. Wrap them in acid-free paper or unbleached muslin, place them in an area with good air circulation, and inspect them regularly.

2 Combining Fabric and Design

Although any garment is the sum of endless decisions both creative and practical, the initial choices concerning fabric and design are the most critical. These choices are essential to the success of the project. It's hard to know whether the process begins with design or fabrication, but the outcome depends upon their compatibility. And that in turn, rests in part with the sewer's familiarity with the fabric. What does the fabric love to do? What does it hate to do? What does it do well? What does it do poorly? Is its texture a significant factor? Every fabric is different, and you must uncover its personality, charms, and strengths and put them to their best use. It's a challenge, to be sure, but an enjoyable and creative one.

The other element of the equation is thorough familiarity with the intended design. Silhouette, the amount of ease built in, the location and number of seamlines, the internal shaping and design details—all need to be assessed. Remember too, that some clothes reveal themselves when they are in motion (think of a pleated skirt, layers, skirt godets, and contrasting linings and facings), so movement is a further consideration. A closely fitted suit changes little in motion, but there is a world of difference with some garments when they hang quietly and when they move.

Be sensitive, too, to the preferences of the intended wearer. Some people prefer the structure of firm fabric and closely fitted clothing, while others like a maximum of ease and a minimum of constriction along with softly flowing fabrics.

Your job—combining fabric with design—will be easier once you've carefully examined both. You'll be educated, and therefore prepared, to match the characteristics of the fabric to the requirements of the design. You'll see how I dealt with this complex subject in the descriptions of the sample garments shown on pp. 19-35.

HOW TO SELECT YOUR FABRIC

Beyond the general concerns listed in the text of Chapter 2, here are some specifics that you need to research when selecting your fabric:

- How does the fabric drape, move, fold, and pleat?

- How will it be cared for?

- How does it respond to heat and moisture?

- Will it shrink?

- Will fraying be a big concern?

- Has a finish been applied to the fabric that will make pressing and even stitching difficult? Will washing help remove the finish? Will it still feel the way you want it to feel?

- Is the fabric so loosely woven that it will become tedious to work with or unmanageable?

- What will the closure be? Will it work with the chosen fabric?

- What sort of buttonholes will work if the fabric is loosely woven?

- Can the fabric bear the strain of pockets?

- Will a lining be necessary?

- Is static likely to be a problem?

- Is perspiration a factor? Cottons and linens are worn in warm climates; will the fabric be too heavy or too stifling?

- Are perspiration marks likely to be visible?

EXAMINING FABRIC

The fabric suggestions on the pattern envelope are a wonderful place to start. But you'll need to go beyond simply accepting those general recommendations—you need to get to know those fabrics, and other possibilities, further. And remember that the suggested fabrics and the amount of ease built into the pattern work together. If the fabric you choose varies significantly from one of the suggested fabrics, be aware that you may need to recalculate the amount of ease and make adjustments in the fit of the garment.

Always work with the best fabric you can find (see pgs. 8 and 11). The fibers will be stronger, the weave better executed, the dyes of a higher quality and better applied, the finishing treatments more carefully and thoroughly affixed. Check that the weave is firm, that the grain is straight, that dyes are well registered.

Be aware of what attracts you to a particular fabric in the first place. Is it the color? The texture? Is it the drape and the hand? You need to be sure that the design you choose will highlight, and not obscure, your favorite features.

Examine the fabric's texture—it may be subtle or bold. It may be a design feature itself—the prominent stripes of an ottoman, the intricacies of a piqué—or it may simply be the medium in which the design is carried out. The smoother and plainer the texture, the less it will distract from details in stitching and seaming. Conversely, the simpler the design of the garment, the more critical the quality of the fabric. The focus will be on it, and it must be able to stand up to the attention it will receive.

Consider also the effect that the inner structure will have on the fabric. How will it feel once interfacing, underlining, facings, and topstitching have been added? Will its basic nature be maintained, or will it become a different fabric?

Heavier fabrics with firm weaves work best in fitted styles, interestingly shaped. Darts, multiple pattern pieces, and curved and shaped seams show up beautifully in firmly woven fabrics, and they help minimize the fabric's bulk. Garment ease is minimal; the silhouette is emphasized.

Fabrics lighter in weight, with a softer hand, are more suited to flowing designs, with less shaping built into the pattern, whose pieces are usually larger and fewer. Lightweight and soft fabrics don't hold design lines very well, so the attention is on the movement of the fabric and the generosity with which it's used, rather than intricate design lines. The fabric itself follows the shape of the body, without the need for complicated shaping and seaming to help it do so. Enough ease needs to be allowed, though, or the garment will seem ungenerous and won't have the fluidity that it needs. More specific considerations are listed in the sidebar on the facing page.

If you're combining fabrics, you need to study more than just their visual compatibility and contrast. Check to see if dyes are colorfast, if the fabrics wash and press similarly, if they stitch together well. If a fabric is sheer, remember that its sheerness is a factor beyond the obvious concerns of modesty. The multiple layers of fabric used in French seams and folded hems will become design lines themselves, which you can use to wonderful advantage.

Take the time to uncover a fabric's personality. Go beyond your initial impressions and presumptions when getting to know a fabric's possibilities. Only then will you truly know it and be able to use it well.

EXAMINING DESIGN

Webster's dictionary defines design as "the arrangement of details which make up a work of art." When choosing a design for your project it's your job to assess the details and how they'll be arranged in your intended design. After carefully examining the fabric, you need to do the same with the design. The perfect fabric will be perfect only if it is paired with the right design, and the most wonderful design will be a disappointment if teamed with an unsuitable fabric.

How many times have you been surprised—pleasantly or unpleasantly—by design details or construction elements that you didn't realize were a part of the pattern, or by an unforeseen alliance of fabric and design? There's more to choosing a pattern than the initial appeal of the fashion drawing or photograph. Although that's usually what attracts us first, it's the line drawings that tell us more. Fashion drawings, and even photographs, can distort the garment. Don't be misled or distracted by a garment's color, fabrication, or even its accessories. Learn more by examining the pattern pieces on the guide sheet. Look at how they're shaped and how they fit together. Examine seams, seam finishes, closures, pockets, and embellishments.

Study what attracts you to a certain design. Is it the overall silhouette, or is it the small details? Is it the movement that the design allows? Is it the hope that it will be flattering, calling attention to certain areas of the body and away from others? Silhouette is a critical factor, and you need to examine the pattern to see how the silhouette is achieved. Does the design need a firm fabric to create the silhouette, or does inner structure play a role? How are shape and movement built into the pattern? Our bodies are shapely, and they move.

Although simple garments with few pieces and straight seamlines are easy to sew, they aren't necessarily attractive or easy to wear. Overly simple designs can lack charm and sometimes do little to flatter the wearer. Beyond silhouette, there are style lines. They build in more than style and visual interest and allow graceful and comfortable movement. They allow the contours of the body to be accommodated in interesting and clever ways. Cotton and linen respond beautifully to sewn-in details like contoured seamlines, interestingly shaped darts, pleats, and godets and the decorative stitching that often accompanies them.

Check the guide sheet to see the amount of ease that's been allowed. It's a critical factor that is all too often overlooked. Garments can be close fitting, fitted, semi-fitted, loose fitting, or very loose fitting. The amount of ease will vary according to style, the drape of the fabric, the way you want the garment to look, and the way you want the garment to feel. The amount of ease is as important as any other design element.

Also factor in the inner structure (interfacing, underlining, shoulder pads, and sleeve heads), as well as surface design details (pleats, godets, topstitching, and closures). These all have a bearing on the fabric's weight, movement, and behavior, and therefore on its design.

Printed fabrics, as well as fabrics with a woven pattern, affect the design. While plain fabrics showcase design details, prints obscure them. Plaids and stripes can enhance design elements—a plaid, used well, can guide the width of pleats, define a hemline, or highlight a waistband, a collar, a cuff, or a pocket. The effectiveness of a plaid or a stripe can be lost though, if the garment sections on which they're placed are too small or if they're juxtaposed in unflattering ways. Use them with care.

In addition to being embellished with applied stitching treatments, fabrics themselves can be manipulated with tucks, pleats, ruching, and shirring. Cottons and linens are naturals for these treatments— the fabrics are easy to manipulate and cooperative to stitch and love to show off surface details.

Design Gallery Patterns

design gallery

Combining fabric and design well isn't alchemy, although it sometimes seems that way. It's the result of careful study and observation. By assessing if the design serves the fabric's requirements, and vice versa, you'll be able to mesh them well. You can then proceed confidently and enjoy the harmonious—and productive—marriage of well-paired fabric and design. Following is a discussion of different garments and a look at how some sample garments have combined design and fabric. ■

shirts

Shirts are the garments that frame the face. They need some structure, but not too much. Almost always worn with another garment, they can be tucked in or out, and they can be belted. If the shirt has sleeves, the sleeves are easy to modify by pushing them up the arms or by rolling up the cuffs. The closure, both on the sleeves and on the front, can be a prominent part of the design. As shirts hang from the shoulders, the fit and support of the garment in that area are critical. Shoulder pads are often needed. It may be difficult to obscure them if the fabric is sheer. (Try covering them with flesh-colored fabric.)

A textured fabric is a good match for a simple style. The pattern of the fabric is more noticeable than it would be with a more complicated design. The understated lines of this blouse work well with the gentle texture of this rose-patterned cotton damask. The bright color was a clue to prewash the fabric to remove excess dye. Although slightly subtler in hue after washing and a little bit softer, the very workable weight of the fabric makes it perfect for a blouse. Too much design interest will overwhelm the texture of the fabric; but to keep the design from being too plain, there's an interesting closure (loops and rose-shaped buttons, which subtly echo the fabric's rose print) and horizontal bands at the hemline and base of the sleeves, adding a little bit of weight and structure. It's a good match of a subtly designed fabric, simple lines, and an interesting detail or two. ■

Cotton organdy is permanently treated to retain its body and loft, and therefore hold its shape. Interfacing in this case is out of the question, as it would be visible, but it isn't really necessary with this firm and bodied fabric. But there needs to be more than a voluminous cloud of brightly colored fabric to define the design. The fabric is transparent, so interest can be derived from (and the silhouette outlined by) the French seams, which will be noticeable, as the fabric will be quadrupled (and opaque) there. This particular blouse deserves its dramatic closure—a big red bow. Even the cuffs have a touch of drama with golden ball buttons fastened like cufflinks. The overall effect: a dramatic fabric used in a bold way. ■

vests

Worn often in warm climates instead of a jacket, which would be too heavy, vests in cotton and linen are a natural choice. Remember that another garment will usually be worn under a vest, so be sure that the garment weights are compatible. Check also that the movement of the underneath garment isn't restricted by the vest, especially at the armscye. A casual garment like a vest often has pockets, so be sure that the fabric can support them. While some vests are structured, others are unstructured. You may need to build in support, keeping in mind that vests hang from the shoulders, so adequate strength in that area is critical.

On a vest, the closure is usually a focal point, so consider what will accentuate the vest the best. Also think about what the vest will be worn with, and gauge its length accordingly.

The dramatic horizontal lines of the ottoman ask for little other than carefully shaped seamlines and a well-defined silhouette. The fabric is stiff and would create a boxlike garment if it were used otherwise. The meeting of the seams at the sides (see the photo below) is an effective detail, while the buttons up the back do their job quietly. Silk organza underlining gives all the inner structure that's needed. In this case, the geometry of the fabric takes the lead and speaks for itself. ■

Well-matched
fabrics and a design full
of interesting details
combine beautifully in
this vest. The subtly
interesting textures
and mix of colors in
the fabrics are echoed
in the abalone buttons.
The vertical band along
the front closure, the
cross ties in the back,
the side slits, the top-
stitching, and the bound
buttonholes all create
interest throughout the
garment. It's best paired
with quiet separates that
stay in the background,
allowing the outfit's
focus of attention to be
the vest. ■

jackets

Jackets, even in cotton and linen, unless unstructured, require inner support. Interfacings can range from lightweight fusibles to firm sew-ins; pockets and plackets and buttonholes need further reinforcement. There may or may not be shoulder pads and sleeve heads, but don't discount these structural tools just because the jacket is made from something other than wool. They can give cotton and linen jackets smart definition and encourage them to maintain a well-defined shape.

The neck edge, center front edges, and hem of a bolero are usually continuous, and though this jacket adds a collar, the multiple rows of topstitching lead the eye around its perimeter. The topstitching and the strength it lends, working in concert with the self-underlining, provide just the right amount of structure. Unsupported, the piqué would have lost its shape; fused, the fabric would have become too stiff. Doubling it with self-fabric provides the perfect amount of support. It's firm enough to hold its shape, and pliable enough to allow movement. There are modest shoulder pads and sleeve heads, just enough to fill out the contours of the jacket. Three-quarter-length sleeves are a summery touch appropriate for the accompanying bare dress. The jacket might have seemed too heavy with full-length sleeves. ■

This fabric is enchanting and it combines two beautifully muted colors, rosy salmon and silvery beige, in an interesting open basketweave. The fibers have been treated to make them lustrous and soft, and the weight is perfect for a jacket. Combining tailored and soft elements, the jacket design has bound buttonholes, welt pockets, a structured collar, and turned-back cuffs with a softly structured flared back. What's missing is stability. The key was to fuse lightweight interfacing to the wrong side of the fabric, meticulously and patiently, keeping the grain in line (the fabric was so loosely woven that it could easily be shifted off grain with the slightest movement of the hands). The fusible also enabled the pockets and buttonholes to be incorporated. They would have been far too risky to attempt had the fabric not been interfaced. The back of the jacket undulates in soft folds, which highlight the luster of the fabric. ■

skirts

A skirt needs to allow a great range of movement. Beyond walking ease, it must accommodate twisting and turning, bending and stretching of the body, all of which involve the waist area. The waistband, or waist area, needs to be sturdy. If it isn't, the skirt will lose its shape, and the engineering of the whole garment will be compromised.

The skirt should be conceived with a top in mind. Whether to include pockets, decorative and/or functional, is also a consideration. If pockets are incorporated into the design, the surrounding area needs to be well structured to keep its shape and bear the strains of the hands, which sometimes rest in the pockets. The length needs to be carefully and patiently determined. Proportion, with the right shoes and accompanying garments, is critical.

The mauve linen, treated to soften it, is woven in an open basketweave pattern. The combination of the weave and the surface treatment makes it attractive but unstable. A fusible, which was used for the matching jacket, would have made the skirt too stiff. Instead, it was carefully cut, controlling the shifting grain, and lined with crepe de Chine. The waistline is faced, and a little subtle topstitching is the only surface treatment. The skirt is a quiet, tasteful, low-key accompaniment to the jacket. ■

The brightly colored floral pattern and the lace trim are lighthearted and call for a design that's similarly so. This medium-weight cotton would normally be too light for a shaped skirt, but using a second layer of the fabric as a facing for the scallops and extending it to the waistline (serving, in effect, as an underlining as well as a facing and a lining) makes it sturdy enough to work. The extra layer also minimizes wrinkling. The lace appliqués at the bottom edge, which are sewn on by hand, add visual distinction and further strengthen the hem area. ■

Although the color of the linen is striking and the texture is pleasant, this skirt needs design interest to lift it above the ordinary. Interesting shaping, topstitching, and seam-related details (in this case, slot seams) are the tools. The slot seams of the pockets incorporate curves, necessitating facings rather than the turned-back seam allowances that most slot seams use. ∎

Plaids are fun to play with, especially when they're teamed up with twin pleats. It takes careful study of the fabric to assess the prominent elements of the plaid and integrate them into attractively framed and spaced pleats. The double pleats of this skirt were created from an underlay; the back edges of the double pleats are stitched along the hem allowance to help them maintain their sharp folds. The skirt's length is determined by the plaid, and its hemline follows a prominent stripe. ■

29

Pleats and gathers control fullness, and so do godets. A sophisticated yet less familiar alternative, godets add swing and an undulating fullness to the hemline. This linen is heavy, and the skirt is shaped with a dozen long, thin panels. The godets, inserted at each seamline, introduce fullness without incorporating excessive weight. The godets are further defined with topstitching. Facings and understitching strengthen the edges of the pockets to prevent stretching and to ensure that they stay flat and don't interrupt the long skirt panels. ■

Cotton and linen dresses range from the highly structured to the loosely shaped—yet what they have in common are fabrics that are comfortable, cool, and easy to wear.

dresses

A classic combination, this fitted sundress features a firm fabric and a shapely, sculpted design. Multiple rows of topstitching highlight and strengthen the front band, the top edges of the pockets, and the hemline. The front band and firm facings along the top edge give the dress the support it needs. ∎

This unimaginably soft pima lawn, woven from the longest and silkiest of cotton fibers, deserves a flowing design. The skirt does simply that. It's cut in a full circle, finished with the narrowest and lightest of machine hems. The bodice is fully lined with cotton batiste, with the lining doing double duty as neck and armhole facings. The fashion fabric was a little too sheer to use as a self-lining: The designs would have shown through, and the color would have been altered. Curved, faced pockets in the skirt, a back zipper, and a self-covered belt are the only other elements. All this fabric wants to do is move gracefully, and this simple design allows it to do just that. ■

32

In this linen shift, a simple silhouette sets off a bold print. A complicated design would have broken up the striking pattern of the fabric; a plain fabric with such a simple design might have lacked interest. In this case, the design steps to the back while the fabric gets most of the attention. Piping, carefully applied so it forms sharp corners, adds interest and structure to the square neckline and armholes; and the side closure, with its bold buttons, is eye-catching. Otherwise the design is simple, choosing to let the attention rest on the fabric. A little interfacing supports the neck and shoulder area. A cotton batiste lining feels soft against the skin, helps lessen wrinkling, and provides just a whisper of structure. ■

33

This sophisticated linen dress combines two matching fabrics—one an all-over cutwork pattern, the other bordered with the cutwork. The bodice is cut from the first—its high boat neck in the front dips to a deep V in the back. Delicate piping defines the neck edge and the waistline. The skirt is full—nearly 6 yd. in circumference—yet the handkerchief linen handles the volume with ease and grace. The skirt's border echoes the cutwork of the bodice. While handkerchief linen might not be the first thought for a wedding gown fabric, this dress shows how successful the combination can be. It's cool, crisp, and elegant, easy to wear, and pretty to look at. Cotton underlines the silk-lined bodice, and the skirt is supported on the inside by a grosgrain ribbon waist stay. Although the skirt is fairly lightweight, it needn't compromise the lines of the bodice by pulling it downward. ■

Trousers, whether formal or informal, demand a great range of movement. They need a sturdy waistband or waistline area that's well supported by inner layers—lack of support in this area will compromise the entire garment.

The weight and the weave of the fabric and the lining and/or underlining are factors. The sturdier the fabric, the better it will maintain the shape of the trousers. Lighter-weight fabrics work better with flowing designs. Almost all pant designs feature pockets, which usually bear great use. They need to be reinforced.

Trousers must be comfortable as well as flattering while the wearer is sitting, standing, and walking. Trousers can be belted or not and cuffed or not. The waistband may be traditional, built-up, or faced. Because of the movement involved, lined trousers usually work best with an independently hemmed lining, which is secured to the seamlines with French tacks.

trousers

This sturdy herringbone weave (a variation of the twill weave, the strongest of weaves) will maintain any shape. Trousers place stresses at the hip crease, across the seat, and at the knees; a strongly woven fabric is needed to stand up to the strain. The contours of the built-up waistband are echoed with topstitching, which helps it keep its shape. ■

3

Equipment and Supplies

One of the joys of sewing with cotton and linen is that little is required in the way of specialized equipment. However, the equipment and supplies that you do use regularly should be first-rate. Your investment in time, money, and the creative process deserves nothing less. You may encounter other challenges as you sew, but putting up with poor equipment shouldn't be one of them. Second-rate equipment will slow you down, and it will compromise your results. Stop battling pins that don't want to pin, thread that kinks and twists, and scissors that don't cut cleanly. The better your equipment, the better your chances for top-notch work.

AT THE MACHINE

Although today's sophisticated machines can do amazing things, it's critical that your **sewing machine** be capable of producing a beautiful, perfectly balanced straight stitch on any fabric or fabric combination.

Correct tension is important for the stitches you see, and it's equally important for all the stitches you don't see. Stitches that are irregular or too loose not only compromise the look of your garment but are also not as strong or as stable as they should be. With linen and cotton's affinity for details, the often-visible stitching that accompanies them needs to be as well defined as possible. Easily controllable or adjustable sewing speed is a must. You'll become frustrated with a machine that lurches or runs away with you when you're trying carefully to control your stitches.

You don't need an extensive collection of **presser feet** for most sewing with cotton and linen. An adjustable zipper foot is a plus (it can be used for piping as well as zippers), a flat felling foot is handy if you plan to do extensive amounts of flat felling, and a foot with a stitch guide is a good idea for accurate placement of surface stitches (although you can usually find an edge on an ordinary presser foot to serve as a guide).

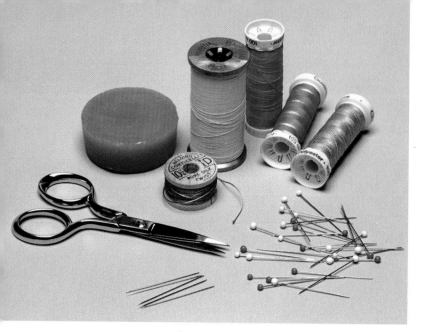

Thin hand needles, 4-in. embroidery scissors, beeswax, top-quality thread, and long pins with glass heads are a few of the notions that will serve you well in working with linen and cotton fabrics.

NOTIONS

Good **pins** are a wonderful ally. Long, thin, sharp ones with glass heads are my favorites. The length will allow you to "double pin," or run the pin in and out of the fabric twice (see the drawing on the facing page). You'll get more mileage and greater stability out of each pin. They'll work harder for you, and the glass heads will make using them easier on your fingers.

Search out the sharpest pins you can find. Some cottons (for example, piqués with their fine filling threads) can be surprisingly hard to pin. Others, because of surface treatments and finishes, can be similarly tough. Get the sharpest, longest, thinnest pins you can find and you'll love them. Discard bent pins. They will never straighten out, and they will distract you while you waste your time digging around for a straight one.

Whatever you do, don't compromise on the quality of the **thread** you use, either for machine or hand sewing. Not only will cheap thread have an uneven appearance and feel, but it will also kink, it will shred in the needle, it won't be strong, and it will be hopelessly frustrating for hand sewing. Buy the best thread you can find. The cost of it is negligible in the overall outlay for any garment you sew. My all-around favorite thread is long-staple polyester, the smoothest and best quality I can find, and I use it for everything except basting (I use silk) and some topstitching. When I want really distinctive topstitching, I use silk buttonhole twist.

Silk basting thread has the advantage of being able to be removed easily (it glides out, unless caught in the machine stitches, in which case it needs a little more encouragement). Further, it won't leave an imprint on your fashion fabric if it's been ironed. Embroidery floss is useful to have on hand for tailor's tacks—it won't be as likely to pull out as other types of thread.

Cotton and linen seldom require thick **machine needles**, and the lighter fabric weights will benefit from the smallest needle you have. Experiment to find what works best. Whenever you sew, first make a fabric sample, layering it exactly the way your garment's fabrics will be layered. Check tension as well as needle size. I start each sewing project with a fresh needle. I can then rest easy, knowing that an inferior needle won't snag the fabric or cause skipped stitches or fraying thread. You may want to try topstitching needles for decorative stitching. They're specially designed with a large eye and a groove at the back of the shank.

Finally, give some thought to your work area, which needs to be well lit. If it isn't, you'll be surprised at the difference that **additional lighting** can make. Also get a good **chair**, and adjust it to the proper height. My comfort level changed hugely for the better when I started using a well-designed office chair with roller wheels. My knees, which I'd been using to push a reluctant wooden chair, no longer hurt. Any office worker (or sewer with a well-designed chair) will echo my sentiments.

Although you may not be doing a huge amount of hand sewing, you do want the hand sewing that you do to be first-rate. You probably have your own favorite **hand needles**. I prefer mine to be long and thin, and able to pierce any fabric without hesitation. Discard your needles the minute they develop a burr or bend, or if the eye shreds your thread. Hand stitching, apart from the coordination involved, is far easier with a needle that suits you (there are hand-sewing needles I love to sew with and hand-sewing needles I hate to sew with).

Beeswax is an old-fashioned sewing staple; you won't use it often, but there's no substitute for it when you do need it. It will strengthen hand-sewing thread, and is therefore used when strength is important: when sewing on buttons, on thread shanks between two buttons to create cufflinks, on thread bars, for sewing on snaps and hooks and eyes. To use it, thread your needle, and pull the thread (usually doubled) through the beeswax a few times. Most beeswax holders have slots for this purpose. Then iron the thread—the heat will melt the beeswax into the fibers, coating them and strengthening them further.

SCISSORS AND CUTTERS

Don't compromise on the quality of your scissors. Superior scissors are essential for the best results. You'll need a variety, including 7-in. or 8-in. bent-handled **shears** for cutting. The long blades will help you achieve smooth cutting lines, and the bend in the handle will allow room for your hand while you hold the blades on the cutting surface. The fabric will get cut, but it won't be distorted. The same shears with micro-serrated blades are fabulous for cutting any fabric with the slightest bit of resistance—they grip the fabric as they cut it. Sharpen or replace your shears the minute they're not razor sharp. Otherwise, you'll pull at the fabric as you cut it, and

DOUBLE PINNING

Double pinning will allow you to get more mileage—and work—out of each pin. The longer your pins are, the better it works.

you'll tire your hands as you try to get your scissors to cut.

Appliqué scissors are useful when you really do need to get up close to the stitching line. I use them for trimming narrow hems and appliqués. Held at an angle, they're also useful for grading seams.

The workhorse scissors in my studio are 5-in. **tailor's point scissors**. They have a sturdy spine, which means they're strong, so I can use them for thick cutting jobs, and their sharp points make them useful for more delicate tasks as well.

I use **embroidery scissors** all the time, but I'm careful not to try to cut anything too thick with them (the blades would soon move out of alignment). Restrict their use to clipping threads, removing stitches, and lightweight cutting jobs that demand accuracy—cutting right into a V, for example, or trimming a single layer of fabric.

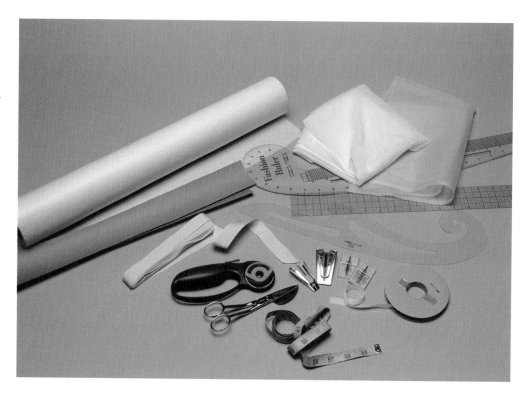

Specialty equipment you will want to keep on hand includes (clockwise from top left): pattern paper, a variety of fusible and sew-in interfacings, French curves and transparent rulers, fusible straight-of-grain stay tape, specialty sewing-machine needles, bias tape makers, a good tape measure, appliqué scissors, a rotary cutter, woven grosgrain ribbon, and strips of brown paper for pressing.

Pinking shears are useful for creating some seam finishes, although a pinked edge is seldom sturdy enough to withstand much wear, especially on a loosely woven fabric. They're useful for softening the edge of interfacing, helping it blend more easily onto the fashion fabric.

A **rotary cutter** is very useful, when used with a transparent ruler for cutting bias strips for facings, binding, pipings, and preparing strips for Hong Kong finishes (see the photo above). Streamlining the process of cutting bias strips will encourage you to use these versatile treatments.

I'm as careful as I can possibly be to avoid cutting over pins, and I cringe if I ever drop my scissors. If they're open when they fall, the blades will get nicked; even if they're closed, they're likely to become misaligned. And I always place them gently on the table for the same reason.

PRESSING EQUIPMENT

The flip side of fabrics that wrinkle easily is that they iron beautifully. Cotton and linen are a pleasure to iron. Although they require a high heat setting, they don't need to be shaped with big amounts of steam and a heavy tailor's iron.

Although I've recently purchased a new steam-generator iron, which I like, I've always been happy pressing cottons and linens with an ordinary **steam iron**. I use either the steam setting or the dry setting and a spray bottle of water. With the spray bottle I can control the amount and location of the moisture, using my hand to shield any areas that I don't want to get wet. My favorite pressing cloth is a big square of silk organza—it's soft, it's transparent, and it can tolerate the hottest settings on my iron, which I need when I'm ironing cotton and linen. Strips of **brown paper** are useful for sliding under seam allowances and facings when you're pressing. This lessens show-through of the seam and facing edges.

As your pressing skills increase, you'll realize how important a good **ironing board** is. It must be well braced, with a broad ironing surface, and be strong enough to withstand the considerable pressure you'll put on it when fusing interfacings. An inexpensive, narrow, wobbly ironing board will frustrate you and compromise your pressing and ironing.

EQUIPMENT FOR PATTERNS AND LAYOUT

I'm devoted to the old-fashioned kind of **tracing paper** that's sold in large sheets. I tape each sheet to a big piece of cardboard or tagboard. I used to roll the sheets up, but they would get more wrinkled with every use. Also, I found I was constantly trying to keep them from rolling up while using them. I'm wary of disappearing tracing paper—apart from the fact that I might not get to it before it disappears, I fear it may leave some sort of residue in the fabric, which could have an effect on the garment later on.

I like a serrated **tracing wheel**—I find it easier to control than the solid-blade type (the one that looks like a pizza cutter). Be sure not to confuse it with a needle-wheel, which is a patternmaker's tool and will be much too harsh for fashion fabrics, especially cotton and linen.

Unbleached muslin is a good staple to have on hand. Its primary use is for making a muslin of your garment—a copy of the garment in something other than the fashion fabric, to allow you to perfect fit and proportion. Muslin has other uses, too—it can be used as a sturdy pressing cloth or a top fabric for a pressing area (over an old blanket or towels). There are also times when it's used as an interfacing or an underlining.

A good **tape measure** is important to have. Get the kind with a set of numbers on both sides, each starting at a different end. It's the easiest tape measure to use, and if you get into the habit of measuring often, the accuracy of your sewing will improve.

A **fashion ruler** and **French curve** are used for altering and refining seamlines and design details. Although you can "eyeball" a lot of lines, they'll be more uniformly curved with these rulers to guide you. A transparent ruler will help you mark topstitching lines and cut bias strips in even widths. Get one that is at least 18 in. long.

As your sewing skills increase, you'll find yourself adapting patterns. Having **pattern paper** on hand will encourage you to cut your own facings, to reshape edges, or to make a full set of pattern pieces when the layout requires it.

MISCELLANEOUS SUPPLIES

Keep a good supply of your favorite **interfacings** and **underlinings** on hand, as well as **shoulder pads** and **sleeve heads**. Having a variety available will encourage you to experiment, and it will save trips to the fabric store.

Bias tape makers are also useful. They come in a variety of sizes. Bias tape has endless uses—facings, piping, binding, decorative seam treatments, Hong Kong finishes. A bias tape maker will ensure prepared bias strips that are consistently folded to an even width.

not removed, these coatings can cause puckering, skipped stitches, and uneven stitching lines.

Fabric with too much dye can be a problem when wearing and caring for a garment. You don't want excess dye rubbing off onto lingerie or at the waistband. Remove all the excess dye you can if you suspect a problem. First soak the fabric in hot water, then cold water, rinsing until the water is clear. Then soak it in a mixture of vinegar and cold water ($\frac{1}{4}$ cup to $\frac{1}{2}$ cup to 1 gal. of water) to set the remaining dye. The fabric may lose a little of its brightness, but you'll be much better off in the long run.

After washing, straighten the grain of the fabric. Check that lengthwise and crosswise grainlines are at right angles. Fabrics often get distorted during their finishing processes or as they're tightly wound onto bolts. Examine the entire piece of fabric—there may be parts of it that are off grain and parts that are on grain. Straighten the grain before pressing—the heat of the iron will help set the grain and make it more difficult to adjust.

I always like to buy a little extra fabric ($\frac{1}{2}$ yd. or so) and suggest you do the same. I like to experiment with fabric treatments, to try out certain seam finishes, interfacings, and stitching details that I might be using in the garment, and to see how the fabric likes to be pressed. My experiments may affect my layout—a certain seam treatment, for example, might require wider-than-usual seam allowances.

Carefully ironing your fashion fabric not only will smooth it out in preparation for layout and cutting but will also give you a lot of useful information. You'll also be able to assess shrinkage and see how the fabric reacts to steam, moisture, and pressure. You'll also detect any imperfections or subtleties in design or weave, and you'll know if both sides of your fabric are identical, if there's an up or down direction, and if heavy pressing flattens out the texture too much.

After the preparation process, you'll be thoroughly acquainted with your fabric and be ready to use it, with all its idiosyncrasies, to its best advantage.

BEFORE YOU SEW

I'm sometimes surprised that sewers don't consider the early parts of the construction process—pattern preparation, layout, cutting, and marking—to be very important. They seem to rush through these tasks until they get to the "real" sewing—stitching on the machine. To me, these early jobs are as critical a part of the real sewing as any other aspect of the garment's construction—in fact, I think of them as more important. Once the layout, cutting, and marking are done, I feel I've gone quite a distance toward completing the project.

Don't underestimate the importance of these steps. Unless they're done with thought and care, the garment won't be a success. No matter how careful your subsequent work, problems will follow if the groundwork hasn't been carefully laid.

Pattern preparation

Carefully cut out each piece of the paper pattern with paper-cutting scissors (paper fibers are surprisingly sharp and strong, and they'll quickly dull your good scissor blades). This is the perfect opportunity to become acquainted with the pattern. How many pieces are there? What is the function of each? How do they go together? How many of each do you have to cut? Which of their markings will have to be transferred to the fashion fabric? How is the grainline placed? Have you made all necessary adjustments to the pattern?

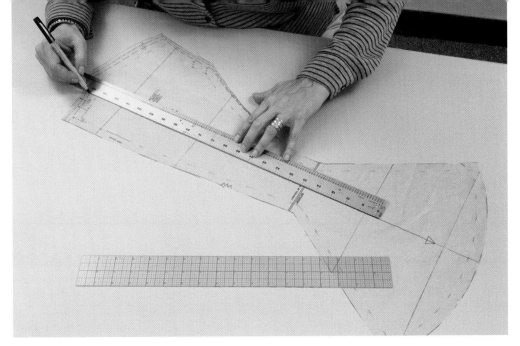

Marking stitching and grainlines (both horizontal and vertical as necessary) will allow you to make the best possible placement of the paper pattern on the fabric.

I mark stitching lines, if they're not already printed on the pattern, and I extend grainlines, if I feel the fabric is slippery and needs particular care with placement. I also draw horizontal grainlines at right angles to the vertical grainlines, if I'm working with plaids, stripes, or a particularly unstable fabric.

You may want to make a full set of pattern pieces—you'll then be able to cut the garment out in a single layer. If your pattern pieces are tissue, you'll easily be able to see any design features through them, and you'll be able to make the best choices in placement. Murphy's Law seems to apply here—prominent designs always seem to end up in the wrong place unless you take the care beforehand to place them exactly where you want them.

Don't be afraid to add facings, interfacings, and underlinings if you feel extra integrity is needed. Remember, the pattern is only a guide, and it can't anticipate all the variations in your fabric's weave, design, and texture, not to mention your own preferred sewing techniques and the result you have in mind.

Layout

By the time you are ready to lay out the pattern pieces, you'll presumably have a thorough overview of the project in your head. You'll have gone through the construction steps, and you'll know how they'll affect layout. Here are some questions to ask yourself at this time:

- *Do you need extra length at the hem?*
- *Will the hem be faced, allowing you to save fabric by shortening the hem allowance?*
- *Do you need extra width at the seam allowances to incorporate a particular finish you've decided upon?*
- *Will facings be cut from the fashion fabric, or are you going to use something lighter in weight and less bulky?*
- *Which pattern pieces can be eliminated?*
- *Which need to be doubled?*
- *Which need to be interfaced or underlined?*

Study the fabric. Check and recheck right and wrong, up and down—sometimes subtleties in weave and design that are barely recognizable at the early stages of working with a fabric become much more noticeable later on. If it's a print, what do you want to emphasize? What do you want to down-

- Hems can be faced.

- Facings don't have to be made out of the fashion fabric.

- You may not have room for one big piece, but you may have room for two smaller pieces. Consider adding a seamline—and incorporating it into your design.

- Instead of a standard waistband, use a facing cut from another fabric for a contour waistband, or face the waistline with a piece of grosgrain ribbon.

- An insertion of another fabric, such as lace, can add length to a sleeve, a skirt, or a torso.

- Use another fabric for the yoke and cuffs.

- See if a center-back seam (and its opening) can be eliminated by having the garment slip over your head. You can either adjust the size of the neckline or shift the opening to the shoulder seam, adding a decorative loop and button closure, for example.

- You may be able to overlap side seams, if they're straight. Side skirt seams can be overlapped, darting from the hipline up to the waistline.

play? This is your chance to put things exactly where you want them.

Cottons and linens often come in widths up to 60 in. If you are used to working with narrow fabrics, you'll find these to be refreshingly wide to work with. Tearing one end of the fabric to establish its grain works well with most cottons and linens, but beware of those with complicated weaves—damask and piqué, for example. They'll resist tearing, and the result will be distorted fabric in the surrounding area.

I like to use a nap layout whenever possible, because there can be subtleties of color and weave that aren't immediately apparent. If I use a nap layout, I know that I won't be surprised later on by any differences.

Check that you've carefully aligned prominent stripes, plaids, and textures. The other day I saw a nicely sewn striped vest that was spoiled by the careless placement of the stripes—they weren't consistent over the princess seams. Use as many pins as you need to match stripes, plaids, and prominent horizontal weaving lines both horizontally and vertically. If you're short on fabric, there are some options you can consider (see the sidebar at left).

If you are going to be cutting two layers at once, be sure both are taut and fully spread out. Little bubbles can easily creep in, especially with lightweight fabrics. Smooth them out carefully, making sure the underlayer is as flat as the top layer. Pin along the selvages to keep the layers together.

Some fabrics are so loosely woven that you can literally shift the grain back and forth with your hand—pulling the fabric to realign grain will be only a temporary solution. With such fabric, be sure that the grain has been shifted to right angles when you lay out and cut your pattern pieces. Be aware that further stabilization will be necessary later on.

To pin the pattern pieces to the fabric, use plenty of pins to minimize shifting, especially with loosely woven cottons and linens. I pin only in the seam allowances if there's the slightest chance that my pins might mar the surface of the fabric or leave any sort of residue behind. As you work, check and recheck the grainlines—nothing is more important at this point. I am scrupulously and continually careful with this—a mistake in grain will undermine the success of the garment.

Consider placing long, straight, on-grain seams along the selvage to save yourself the trouble of finishing the seam allowance. Check, though, to make sure the weave isn't overly tight along the selvage, and be aware that the effect can extend 2 in. to

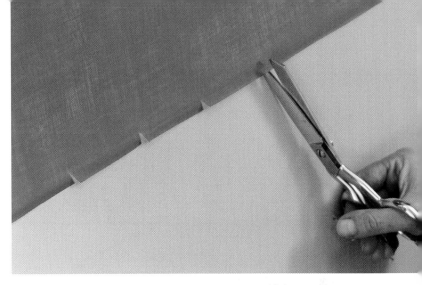

Nicking a selvage can release some of the tightness along the edge of some fabrics.

3 in. into the body of the fabric. Cutting off the selvage can help, as can placing the pattern pieces some distance in from the selvage. If you don't have fabric to spare, you can try releasing some of the tightness by making small nicks in the selvage (see the photo at right). If the tightness is considerable and no allowances have been made for it, your seams will be forever puckered, and no amount of careful stitching and pressing will straighten them out.

Leave wider-than-usual seam allowances when working with loosely woven or especially ravelly fabrics, if possible. They'll ravel during construction and will need to be tidied up. It's important to be able to cut off what's frayed and still have a reasonable seam allowance.

Border prints are usually printed along the selvage edge. If the fabric is tightly woven, then the consequences of shifting from the vertical grain to the horizontal grain will be minimized. Work with a full set of pattern pieces to best assess placement and get the most mileage out of your border print.

Finally, don't be afraid to play around with layout. I seldom use the layout recommended in the pattern. I love the challenge of being able to come up with the best layout possible for my unique demands on the pattern. I'm convinced there's always a workable solution; it's just up to me to find it. Challenge your creativity—you'll discover innovations that normally wouldn't have occurred to you, and your garment may well improve as a result.

Cutting

With particularly slippery or hard-to-tame fabrics, smaller pieces are easier to deal with than larger pieces. If I can, I cut the fabric into smaller sections. I often map out a general layout first, making sure I'll have enough room for everything, then I cut the fabric into smaller pieces for the actual pattern-piece placement, pinning, and cutting.

It's easier to control a smaller piece of fabric with a few pattern pieces. A large piece of fabric that slides off the cutting surface, distorting the fabric as it falls, makes for inaccurate and frustrating cutting. If you do have to keep the fabric in one piece, find some support for the fabric that doesn't fit on your cutting surface—the backs of a couple of chairs or another table, for example. Although cutting fabric into smaller pieces for the sake of layout accuracy and ease may seem extravagant, it makes sense when weighed against the advantages of greater control and accuracy.

I like to cut fabric with bent-handled 7-in. or 8-in. dressmaker's shears with good, sharp blades. If I've placed any alignment pins in the fabric, I check carefully that they're not in the path of my scissors. Bent-handled shears will cause the least disturbance to your fabric as you cut. The blades will stay on the cutting surface, level with the fabric, and the bent handles will allow room for your hand. Dull blades will distort the fabric and sabotage your careful layout, and they're very tiring to use. Sharp scissors make cutting far more efficient and successful.

You may want to invest in micro-serrated shears. They grip wonderfully as you cut; I'm so fond of my pair that I use them for most big cutting projects, slippery or not.

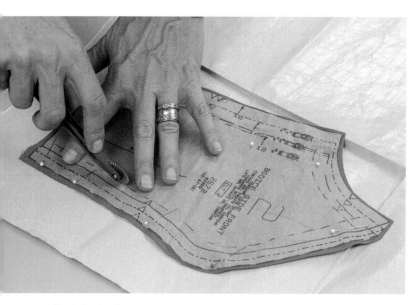

Rock the tracing wheel back and forth, using short strokes. With your free hand, flatten the fabric as you work.

kind, and the new no-wax tracing paper that has a powdery feel to it. With the latter, you have to be careful because the powder comes off very easily. I'd use it judiciously and be watchful that it doesn't end up anywhere but where you want it to.

Before using carbon paper, check to make sure it will show up enough, but not too much. Mark only as strongly as you have to—it's better to struggle to see faint marks than to ruin your fabric with heavy marks. Lighter is better. The marks mustn't show through to the right side of the fashion fabric, and the tracing wheel mustn't make lasting and noticeable impressions. Be sure to check the tracings' reaction to ironing—sometimes the marks almost disappear when ironed, but sometimes they intensify. One advantage (among many) of using an underlining is that the carbon marks go onto the underlining, which is then joined to the fashion fabric; the fabric is spared from being directly marked.

I know that when I use them, the fabric will stay right where I want it to.

Then, using plenty of pins, cut the fabric. Use wider-than-regular seam allowances for edges prone to fraying and as required for special seam or seam-allowance treatments. Have your cutting surface placed so you can get at it from all sides. Reposition yourself, not the fabric, as you cut.

Once it has been cut, handle the fabric as little as possible until it has been stabilized. You may want to strengthen certain edges temporarily—the top edge of a skirt, for example—with a wide machine zigzag.

Marking

Once cut, your pattern pieces may be ready for assembly, or they may require some marking. You can mark notches by making little clips into the seam allowance, you can mark them with stick-on symbols, or you can use tailor's tacks. The most thorough method, though it's slightly time-consuming, is to mark with dressmaker's carbon. There are a number of types of tracing paper available—the old-fashioned wax kind (my favorite), the disappearing

There are a number of methods for applying the marks to the fabric, depending on the way the garment has been cut:

- *If a garment section has been cut in a single layer, right side up, with the pattern tissue on top, simply put the tracing paper underneath and trace. The carbon will mark the wrong side of the fabric.*
- *If there are two layers, with the right sides of the fashion fabric on the outside, slide a folded piece of carbon paper, carbon sides out, between the layers (you'll have to remove some of the pins). Trace; the carbon will mark both sides on the inside (the wrong side).*
- *If there are two layers, with the wrong sides of the fashion fabric on the outside, sandwich them in a folded piece of carbon paper, carbon sides in (again, you'll have to remove some of the pins). Trace; the carbon will mark both sides on the outside (the wrong side).*

My favorite method is a little different, and although it calls for an extra step, it makes up in accuracy what it loses in speed. Start with two layers of fabric, wrong sides out and the pattern tissue pinned on top; place them on top of a single thickness of carbon paper, its right side up. Trace as necessary; you'll be marking the bottom layer only. Move the fabric away from the carbon for a minute and remove the pattern tissue, but put the pins back into the two layers of fabric right away. Flip the two layers of fabric over, and you'll see the traced lines you just made. Not only are they the markings you need, they are also your new tracing guidelines. Return the fabric to the carbon without the paper pattern, and trace over the marks. You now have two accurately marked garment sections, with none of the shifting and discrepancies that other methods of marking can lead to.

When using the tracing wheel, rock it back and forth as you trace, using short strokes, rather than a long, uninterrupted motion. Use your free hand to smooth out the fabric as you go along (see the photo on the facing page). The fabric will stay under the wheel rather than creep ahead and become distorted.

If you are using interfacing, you'll need to mark that, too. Be sure you keep grainlines as they should be when you're joining layers, whether by hand or machine or by fusing. You may need to refer back to the pattern tissue for accurate grain placement.

You may want to add further clarity by going over some of your traced marks with basting thread (see the photo at right). While the carbon tracings mark the inside of the fabric, there are times when you need to see the marks on the outside. A quick row of hand basting will save you endless flipping of the garment sections, trying to see where something is marked. Marking with pins usually doesn't work because they fall out all too easily. Basting is quick and accurate. Use a contrasting thread, but on white or light-colored fabric, make sure to use a pastel. You'll still be able to see it, but the thread's color won't come

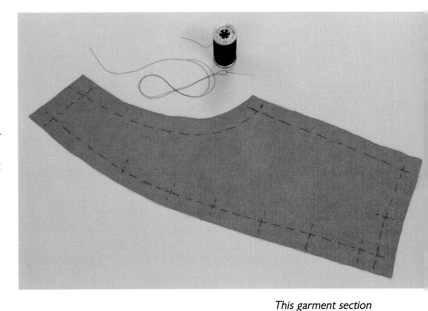

This garment section has been carbon-traced and then thread-basted to make the markings stand out and be visible on both sides.

off on the fabric. Silk basting thread (not buttonhole twist or waxed silk tailor's basting thread) is a pleasure to work with, and has the advantage of not leaving an imprint when pressed.

Obviously there are times when you needn't be so careful with your marking. Carefully cut seam allowances on trousers and skirts are usually sufficient as guidelines, just as long as you have marked—in some fashion—any important details and placement lines. You want to know exactly where to sew; it shouldn't be a matter of guesswork.

Don't underestimate the importance of careful marking. I'm very dependent on what my fabric tells me; I'd feel as if I were starting off on a trip without a road map if I didn't prepare my fabric thoroughly. Your goal is accuracy, and only with the help of clear, well-applied markings can you ensure it. There is no substitute for these important steps. Their careful completion is as essential to the finished garment as anything else you do later.

5 | Sewing Techniques

The level of sewing can easily be elevated by using a little extra care. Redo a crooked row of stitching, baste before you sew, pin carefully, measure accurately, and press patiently. The smallest of details combine to make a garment a technical success.

Sew with your head, first and foremost, and become a shrewd observer of your work. Know when it's right, and know when it needs a little more effort. Learn to take delight in the decision-making process—it is as important to the creative process as designing the perfect sleeve or matching pattern to fabric. There are endless technical decisions before you—which seam width? which closure? where to put interfacing, and which one to choose? Try to get in the habit of weighing the possibilities, reviewing their pros and cons, and assessing the results of your actions.

BASTING

I urge you to get reacquainted with the concept of basting, both as a preliminary step to mark placement lines and other important information and later to join garment sections together before stitching (see the photo on p. 52). It's quick and easy to do, and there are instances when no amount of careful pinning (and hoping for the best) can give you the control that the basting does. Try it—I think you'll be amazed at the difference it can make.

MATCHING

Properly lined-up joinings can be a visual delight, just as poorly lined-up joinings can be jarring. It's worth the extra care to get them right. The process starts with careful cutting and marking, then measuring, machine (if not hand) basting, then stitching. Be prepared to stitch again if the results are less than perfect.

To line up an intersection, put a pin perpendicular to the stitching line, and offset the join slightly to counteract the pressure of the foot. The foot will push the top layer toward you a little bit, so push it back a tiny fraction before you sew. The layers should be evened out during the stitching.

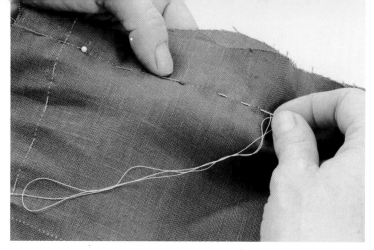

Garment sections joined by basting will not shift around during stitching, as they might if only pins were used.

On the machine, a basting stitch (or the machine's largest stitch) can be a useful first step in joining plaids, stripes, and anything else that must match up (decorative seams, for example). Although the basting holds layers securely, it allows for the minute adjustments that make for perfect alignment. A stitch or two of the basting can be cut, if necessary, and the layers can be realigned. Sometimes there's enough flexibility in the stitching that nudging the fabrics and re-pinning are enough to ready them for the permanent row of stitching, echoing the basting row.

DIRECTIONAL STITCHING

Fabric derives its strength from the intersections between its lengthwise and crosswise threads. It stands to reason then, that when fabric is cut off-grain (that is, not along the horizontal or vertical grainlines), the wide end, where there are more intersections, would be stronger than the narrow end, where there are fewer intersections.

Picture an A-line skirt. The fabric is stronger (there's more of it) at the hem edge than at the waistline edge. So, rather than starting to sew the side seam at the waist, where the fabric is narrower and less stable, start sewing at the bottom edge, where the fabric is wider and stronger. Wider to narrower is the rule.

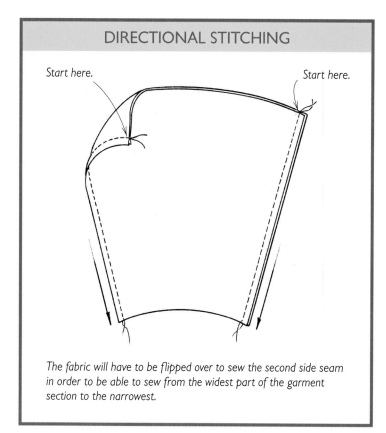

The fabric will have to be flipped over to sew the second side seam in order to be able to sew from the widest part of the garment section to the narrowest.

If you were to start sewing at the weaker (narrower) end of a piece of fabric, it would be likely to distort along the seamline (from being handled and pinned, and from the pressure of the presser foot). Those distortions would carry through the entire seamline. However, by starting at the stronger (wider) end of the fabric, its overall strength will help stabilize the seamline as the fabric narrows and weakens.

MEASURING

When doing pattern work, you often have to figure out measurements by multiplying and dividing, and when you do, working with fractional inches can be extremely tedious. My advice is to use centimeters instead of inches. It's much easier to divide 107 cm by 10 (for preparing a scalloped border, for example) than it is to divide 47¼ in. by 10. So, although you may not customarily work in the metric system, you might want to switch from time to time. Most tape measures have centimeters as well as inches on at least one side.

HAND STITCHES

Although many garments can be sewn entirely by machine, others make frequent use of hand stitching. It's a good idea to brush up on your hand stitches, so you'll be well informed when it comes time to choose them and use them. Here are a few of the most common:

Hand basting Hand basting is a simple running stitch, whose size varies according to use; the smaller it is, the more secure it is. Using a single thread in a contrasting color (avoid dark thread on a light-colored fabric; use a pastel instead), make a running stitch to go over seamlines, pocket placement lines, button and buttonhole placement lines, hemlines, waistlines, and armscyes. Use hand basting wherever definition and placement are important. Basting also joins garment sections accurately in preparation for machine stitching.

Hand overcasting The least obtrusive of seam-allowance finishes, hand overcasting leaves a single row of thread at the raw edge. There are times when any other seam-allowance finish is overpowering, and the gentle presence of hand overcasting is called for.

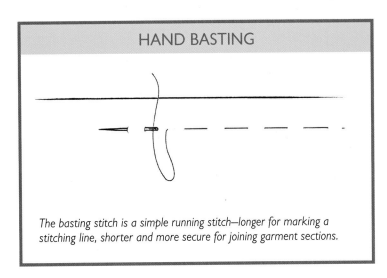

HAND BASTING

The basting stitch is a simple running stitch—longer for marking a stitching line, shorter and more secure for joining garment sections.

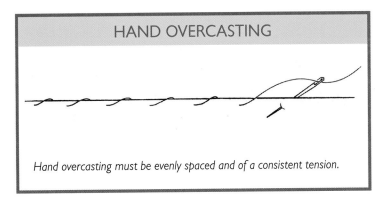

HAND OVERCASTING

Hand overcasting must be evenly spaced and of a consistent tension.

Catchstitch Distributing the tension of the stitch well and eliminating any pulling, the catchstitch holds seam allowances and overlapping layers flatly in place.

Backstitch The sturdiest of the hand-sewing stitches, the backstitch is strong enough to sew in sleeves and to join bodices to skirts. Although not often used with cotton and linen, it's useful to know. Use double thread, waxed, for greatest strength.

Prick stitch The prick stitch is a variation of the backstitch, in which the length of the stitch on the surface is shortened so that it appears as a tiny dot of thread. Like

CATCHSTITCH

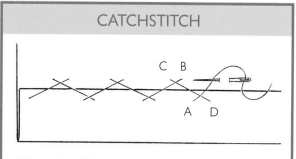

The stitch itself proceeds from left to right, although the needle is pointed to the left. The needle goes in twice for each stitch, once at the top (from B to C) and once at the bottom (from D to A). On a hem, the distance BC would be minimal.

BACKSTITCH

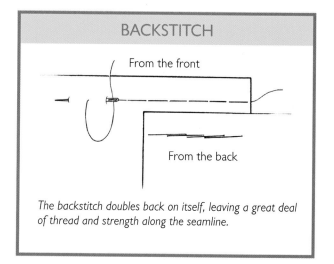

From the front

From the back

The backstitch doubles back on itself, leaving a great deal of thread and strength along the seamline.

PRICK STITCH

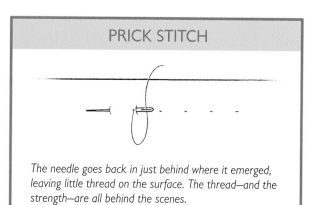

The needle goes back in just behind where it emerged, leaving little thread on the surface. The thread—and the strength—are all behind the scenes.

FELL STITCH

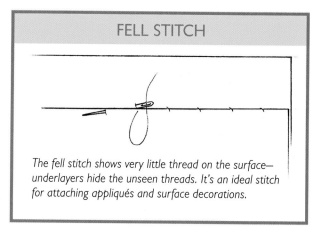

The fell stitch shows very little thread on the surface—underlayers hide the unseen threads. It's an ideal stitch for attaching appliqués and surface decorations.

the backstitch, it's strongest when worked with waxed double thread.

Fell stitch The fell stitch is used to sew the lining around the zipper opening and is often used to sew in jacket linings (if they've not been sewn in by machine). It's also used to attach trims and appliqués to the surface of the fabric. Strong and unobtrusive, the fell stitch leaves barely a trace of thread on the surface. There must be an underlayer, though, in which to bury the thread at the back of the stitch.

Slipstitch Slipstitch is a stitch in which the thread is hidden in the channel formed by a fold—usually a hem fold or a bias binding fold. The needle appears briefly to catch a thread of the underlayer, then goes back inside the fold. It's not a strong stitch, but strength isn't always the primary concern when holding layers together. Most cotton and linen hem allowances are lightweight, though, and simply need to be held gently in place.

Slip basting This is a basting technique that is worked from the right side of the garment. The seam allowance of one side is turned under along the seamline and pinned in place along the matching seamline. A row of slipstitches joins the layers together at the seamline. Although invisible from the right side, the slipstitches are

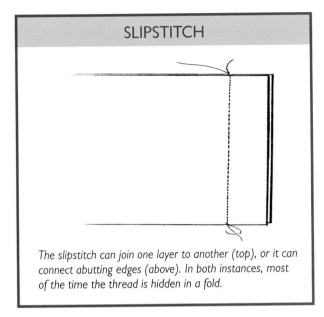

SLIPSTITCH

The slipstitch can join one layer to another (top), or it can connect abutting edges (above). In both instances, most of the time the thread is hidden in a fold.

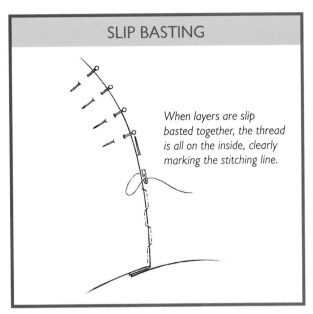

SLIP BASTING

When layers are slip basted together, the thread is all on the inside, clearly marking the stitching line.

visible from the inside, clearly and accurately marking the stitching line. Slip basting is especially useful when matching stripes and plaids.

PRESSING

Pressing is an often underappreciated part of the construction process. It's easy to underestimate its importance and the contribution it can make to a beautifully sewn garment. If you did some preliminary testing (see pp. 42-44), your fabric's peculiarities and idiosyncrasies will have been revealed to you—its preferences in temperature, moisture, and pressure. By this time you know what works best—a dry iron with a damp pressing cloth, a steam iron with no pressing cloth, or a steam iron with a pressing cloth. All are possibilities, but you won't know the best choice unless you experiment. With linen and cotton, there are too many variations in texture, dyes, weave, surface treatment, and fiber content—not to mention your own pressing equipment—to be able to predict any fabric's reaction to heat and moisture.

You may use a gravity-feed iron, you may use an iron with a steam generator, or you may use a simple iron with or without a steam setting. If your iron doesn't produce steam, you'll need to create it somehow. Cotton and linen need both high ironing temperatures and moisture. I rely on a spray bottle filled with water, which allows me to control the amount of moisture as well as its exact placement. If I had an enormous amount of cotton and linen to iron, I'd certainly prefer a steam iron, but for the close and careful pressing that garment construction requires, a dry iron with a spray bottle and a pressing cloth is a workable option. My favorite pressing cloth is a soft square of silk organza. Sometimes I apply the water directly to the fashion fabric, sometimes I spray the pressing cloth. You'll have to experiment to see which works best.

Pressing vs. ironing

Pressing and ironing are not the same thing, and you need to understand the distinction. Pressing involves downward pressure. Its goal is to flatten layers and to make something stay as manipulated with the aid of pressure, heat, and steam. Ironing involves moving the iron back and forth, usually with the goal of smoothing out the fabric and removing wrinkles. Ironing has the potential to stretch and distort fabric, so iron judiciously. While most work with the iron involves a combination of the two techniques, be aware of their differences. It's mainly pressing that's used during the construction process, the fashion fabric having been ironed—carefully—beforehand.

Certainly, careful pressing will improve the appearance of your finished garment, but it is also an ongoing part of the construction process. Apart from its continuing role in pressing seam allowances and flattening layers, there will be sections of the garment that you won't be able to get at once it's finished. Get used to pressing carefully and continuously.

Pressing seams

When treating a just-sewn seam, your first step is to meld the stitches, by pressing the seam flat—not open yet, just flat. You're not ironing—ironing involves moving the iron back and forth on the fabric—you're pressing your iron down, flat onto the fabric, with a generous amount of pressure. Don't overlook this important step. I know that it seems that melding the stitches would have little impact, but that's not true—it lays the groundwork for a beautifully pressed seam.

Next, spread the seam allowances open and press. I like to spread them open with my fingernails—it's almost as if I'm scratching the seamline—doing a few inches at a time, working my way up the seam (I usually work from right to left, up the ironing board). Spreading the seam allowances carefully before pressing the seam eliminates the possibility of pressing in those narrow little creases that parallel the seam. Once pressed, they can be stubborn to remove, and it's much easier to avoid the

problem from the start. If there's any curve at all, press the seam on a curved surface and clip as necessary to allow the seam allowances to flatten out.

I use a silk organza pressing cloth when I'm pressing the right side of the fabric. Certain fabrics are easily glazed or scorched. You should be careful with linens, as their natural wax content makes glazing a tendency. Some textured fabrics are easily flattened out. If this seems to be a problem, try pressing the fashion fabric right side down into a thick terry towel to absorb its texture. After pressing, allow the fabric to cool before you move it, especially if a fusible interfacing has been applied. I like to use starch when pressing linen garments, but it does sometimes get sticky if you press too soon after spraying. Let the starch soak into the garment for a minute or two, and the tendency will be diminished.

If I'm doing a lot of careful pressing on a small garment section, I set up a little pressing area at my worktable—I pad the surface with a few towels and a layer of muslin. There's no need to keep running to the ironing board if I can do my ironing in a more accessible place. And I'm sometimes able to get up closer to it and direct more light on it than I can if I'm standing up at an ironing board, some distance from good lighting. I find that if I take my iron elsewhere, I can have all the light I need, exactly where I want it.

When pressing a faced edge, open out the to-be-folded seam first. Press the seam allowances open, then press them toward the facing, then fold the edge and press it. In addition to helping flatten out internal layers, this will allow you to control the fold—favoring it to one side or the other as you wish—and it will eliminate a pressed-in trough along the fold line. Curved faced edges are a little trickier; see the sidebar on the facing page.

Curved faced edges are difficult to press—the curve is often marred by visible corners and detectable inner clips in the seam allowance. The corners are formed where clips have been made, weakening the fabric's structure and releasing its tension, encouraging it to cave in. But if you establish the curve before you clip, you'll end up with a smooth curves whose clips are undetectable.

If the curve is wide—a neckline curve, for example—open out the facing and try to press the seam allowances open. It will be difficult, as you won't be able to flatten it, but work your way along the seamline, pressing it a little bit at a time. Use a ham, a pressing mitt, or the tip of your sleeve board to help you. Then press the seam allowances toward the facing. Again, it will be difficult, but work along, slowly and carefully. Then fold the facing in place, and press the neck edge from the facing side, favoring the seamline so that it falls to the inside of the garment. Finally, clip the seam allowance as necessary, staggering the clips so that different layers are trimmed in different places (see the drawing at right). You'll have a beautifully curved seamline, without a hint of corners.

It's a little more difficult with smaller curves—scallops, for example—but if you're able to get the point of your iron into the curve and establish it before clipping, you'll improve your result. There may not be enough room to be able to spread out seam allowances, but you will be able to press them toward the facing. Use care, though—curved edges incorporate a variety of grains, and you don't want to cause distortion by pressing too strongly along unstable edges, especially with the point of your iron. ■

The fashion fabric is favored toward the inside of the garment to keep the facing from being seen. Pressing the fabric in this way makes it easier to achieve a smooth curve.

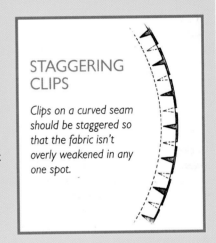

STAGGERING CLIPS

Clips on a curved seam should be staggered so that the fabric isn't overly weakened in any one spot.

SEAMS

Beyond holding garment sections together with the correct choices in thread and stitch length, seams can easily become a decorative focus. Cotton and linen present a wonderful backdrop for details, both dramatic and subtle, and the ease with which they can be created makes them even more appealing. There's a wealth of decorative seam treatments. You'll find them fun to incorporate into your design, easy to do, and rich in impact.

Seam treatments and finishes can add a dash of the unexpected—a sporty flat-fell seam on a cotton organdy evening shirt, for example, or slot seams that hide buttonholes, or French seams on a transparent fabric that double as sharply etched design lines. Cotton and linen behave so well when they're being stitched, and press so beautifully, that it's almost a shame to make a cotton or linen garment that doesn't take advantage of the affinity that these fabrics have for stitching-related details.

- Slip-baste if there are stripes or plaids that need to be perfectly aligned (see the photo below).
- As you machine-stitch, pull the fabric gently from both the top and bottom if the seam appears to be puckering.

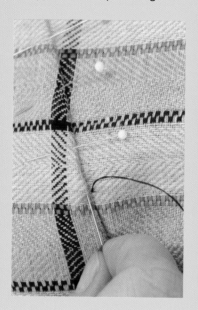

Slip-baste plaids so patterns align perfectly.

- Backstitching is rarely necessary, especially if the seam will be crossed with another or if it will be secured later. It will distort the layers, and it's often difficult to backtrack exactly on the stitching line. If you prefer more security than simply sewing to the end of the seamline, shorten your stitches as you near the end of the seamline (see the drawing at right). (You can also begin with short stitches, and increase to your desired stitch length once you are past the first 1 in. or so.)
- Lift your presser foot frequently, if it seems to be shifting the top layer of fabric. If the problem is severe, hand-baste the seam first. ▪

AN ALTERNATIVE TO BACKSTITCHING

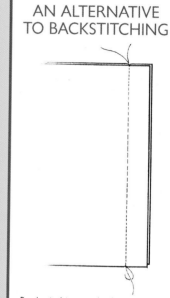

Backstitching at the beginning and end of a seamline is rarely necessary—it causes puckering and stiffness and is seldom accurate. Shortening the stitch length is adequate.

Seams that incorporate additional rows of stitching are truly effective only when that stitching is perfectly straight and even. Experiment with different types of thread, needle size, stitch length, and stitch placement. It's the only way to be sure you'll be happy with the outcome. Don't rely on guesswork for these most visible of details; see the sidebar above for some hints on getting the best results.

If the grains of the garment sections you're stitching together aren't the same, always sew with the weaker grain on top (see the drawing on the facing page). On a princess seam, for example, you'll sew one seam top to bottom (left side front on top of the center front, starting at the top) and the other bottom to top (right side front on top of the center front, starting at the bottom). Since the weaker grain is the less stable, that's the one that is more likely to shift and slip. If it's on top, you are better able to control it, by careful pinning, stitching, and, if necessary, basting.

Always experiment with the same layering that you'll be using in your garment. If interfacing has been incorporated into the seamline, put that into your experimental seam too, and make your test seam long enough and wide enough—at least 12 in. long by 4 in. wide—to assess the results accurately (see the photo on the facing page). When you purchase your fabric, be sure to get extra yardage for experimentation. And when you're laying out and cutting, be sure to increase seam allowances as necessary for decorative seam and seam-allowance treatments.

Experiment with thread—a good quality long-staple polyester works beautifully with most cottons and linens. If you choose top-stitching thread for the additional rows of stitching that many of these seam treatments require, use it for the top thread only; use your regular thread in the bobbin. Test to check that the tension is as you want it—none of the bottom thread must be visible. Remember that seams that incorporate multiple rows of stitching are difficult, and sometimes impossible, to alter later.

Most important, seam treatments that involve manipulating the seam allowance and adding extra rows of stitching will strengthen the seam, but they will also stiffen it, affecting the garment's hang and drape. This may be exactly the effect you're after, or it may not. Bear that in mind when you're experimenting with and choosing seam and seam-allowance treatments.

DECORATIVE SEAMS

There are a number of classic seam treatments that suit cotton and linen perfectly, for these fabrics fold well, they stay in place once folded and pressed, and the extra rows of stitching that these decorative seams entail show up beautifully.

Flat fell

The flat-fell seam is wonderfully sturdy, and flat is what it is. It can incorporate a degree of curve in the seam, and it's versatile enough to work with the sheerest to the heaviest of fabrics (denim jeans are sewn with flat-fell seams).

The flat-fell seam is a well-controlled combination of seam and seam finish—but it

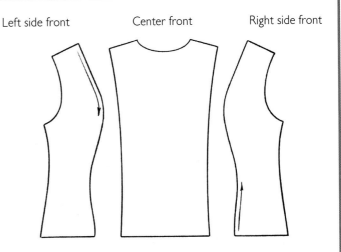

SEWING WITH THE WEAKER GRAIN ON TOP

Left side front   Center front   Right side front

The relatively straight side seams of the center front are more stable than the matching curved seams of the side fronts. Therefore the side-front pieces need to be topmost when the seams are stitched. One seam will be sewn top to bottom; the other will be sewn bottom to top.

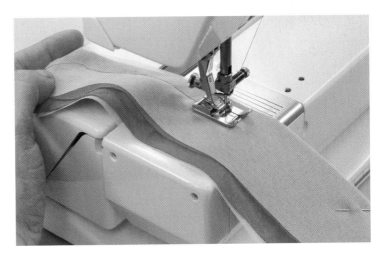

It's critical to sew a test seam before you work on your garment. Arrange the fabrics and any inner layers in the same order as the seam to be stitched.

does result in a seam that's four layers thick. Be aware of its effect on your fabric's color, drape, and fluidity. A sheer fabric won't be sheer at all if four layers of it are used, nor will it drape and flow the way it would with an ordinary straight seam. You may, in fact, choose it because of the strength it adds to the seamline.

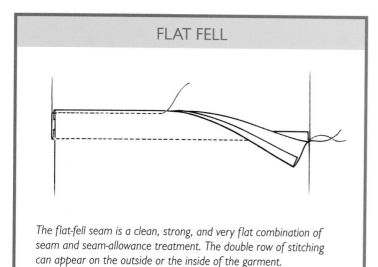

FLAT FELL

The flat-fell seam is a clean, strong, and very flat combination of seam and seam-allowance treatment. The double row of stitching can appear on the outside or the inside of the garment.

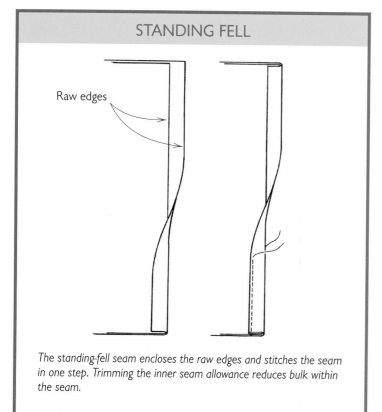

STANDING FELL

Raw edges

The standing-fell seam encloses the raw edges and stitches the seam in one step. Trimming the inner seam allowance reduces bulk within the seam.

The flat-fell seam shows one row of stitches on one side, and two on the other. Although we're accustomed to seeing the double-stitched side on sportswear, either can appear on the right side of the garment. If this is a technique you plan to use often, you may want to invest in one or more flat-felling feet (they come in a variety of widths). Cotton and linen are so cooperative to work with, however, that you may not find it necessary to use a special foot.

To make a flat-fell seam, sew both layers together along the seamline. Then trim one seam allowance and wrap the other over it, folding the raw edge inside; then stitch it into place along its folded edge. If you want two rows of stitching on the outside, then sew wrong sides together; if you want one row of stitching on the outside, sew right sides together. Be sure there is no shifting of the wrapped seam allowance; tiny diagonal drag lines will develop and spoil the clean effect.

Standing fell

The standing-fell seam is similar to, but weaker than, the French seam. It's similar to a bound seam, but it's done all in one step, with a single row of stitching. One edge is trimmed to be very narrow, and the other, wider edge wraps around it and is machine stitched. It's not a particularly strong seam, but not all seams are subjected to significant—or even moderate—strain.

French seam

A French seam is gorgeous when it's the perfect width, when it's been carefully pressed, and when seam allowances are absolutely even and cleanly stitched. When using a French seam for sheer garments, remember that the seam allowance, once finished, will consist of four layers of fabric. French seams are particularly striking when used with a sheer fabric; the seam allowances will stand out in sharp contrast to the rest of the garment.

To stitch a French seam, first calculate the desired finished width and double it. Depending on your fabric, add a little extra to accommodate the turn of the cloth (the fabric that is lost in the fold). The thicker the fabric, the greater the allowance. Put wrong sides together, and stitch halfway between the raw edge and the seamline. Press the seam (unopened) to meld the stitches, then press the seam open. Then fold the seam carefully, exactly along the seamline, the raw edges to the inside. Trim any frayed edges, and enclose the raw edges with the second row of stitching. Press to meld the stitches again, and finally, press the seam allowance in the desired direction.

French seams can be tiny—as narrow as ⅛ in. If your French seam is this narrow, be sure the weave of the fabric can tolerate such a narrow seam without being weakened or destabilized. Be sure you've adequately trimmed and completely enclosed the raw edges inside your second row of stitching—if you haven't, they'll form an unattractive fringe that is impossible to trim once the seam has been stitched.

False French seam

A false French seam looks similar to a regular French seam (they both enclose raw edges), except that a row of stitching is visible along the outer edge of the seam allowance. To make a false French seam, simply sew a regular seam, trim the seam allowances evenly, then fold them in. Finish by stitching the seam allowances together close to the folded edge.

Slot seam

Slot seams are easy, fun, and just the sort of detail that shows up so well in cotton and linen. They can be very subtle or very dramatic, and apart from decorating seamlines, slot seams can expand their role by

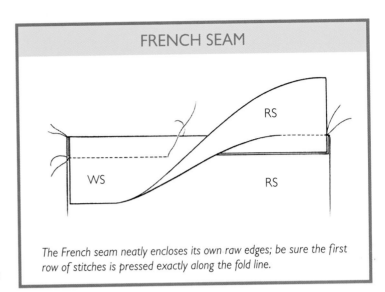

FRENCH SEAM

The French seam neatly encloses its own raw edges; be sure the first row of stitches is pressed exactly along the fold line.

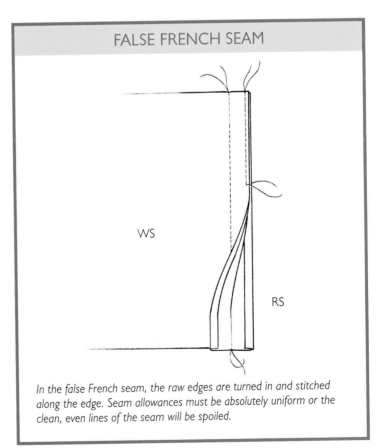

FALSE FRENCH SEAM

In the false French seam, the raw edges are turned in and stitched along the edge. Seam allowances must be absolutely uniform or the clean, even lines of the seam will be spoiled.

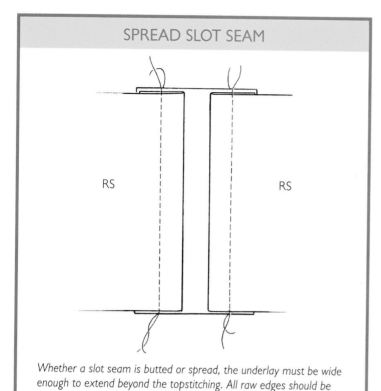

SPREAD SLOT SEAM

RS   RS

Whether a slot seam is butted or spread, the underlay must be wide enough to extend beyond the topstitching. All raw edges should be finished, either before or after stitching the underlay.

Slot seams form pockets on this blue linen skirt.

incorporating pockets and buttonholes. A horizontal slot seam with pockets on the dropped waist of a linen skirt is a wonderful look (see the photo below), as is a tailored jacket with a series of horizontal slot seams on the bodice front, each revealing a buttonhole.

The slot seam is an open welt seam—and the slot opening can be butted or spread. If spread, the color, texture, and grain of the underlay can add further interest. Slot seams work anywhere—horizontally or vertically, discreetly or boldly placed. However, they are best avoided in sheer fabric—the work behind the scenes will be too visible and will distract from the charm of the open seams.

To make a butted slot seam, baste the seam closed, press it open, center the underlay, and stitch each edge of the underlay to the turnback. Then topstitch on either side of the center of the seam and remove the basting. If a bias underlay is used, stabilize it with a lightweight interfacing to eliminate distortion. For a pocket, a pocket bag can be attached to the facings of a slot seam. For a buttonhole, an underlay (or facing) with a machine buttonhole can be placed underneath a small opening in a slot seam (the actual opening in the slot seam is difficult to reinforce sufficiently to serve as the real buttonhole).

Although slot seams are easiest to do when the seamline is straight, they can be added to curved seamlines (see the photo on the facing page), in which case they will need to be faced. Be aware of the bulk this will add and decide if it's still a workable choice. Also, if you face a curve, be sure that the edge of each seam is perfectly turned. This seam, like so many similar treatments, is stunning when impeccably sewn but loses much of its impact if the turning and stitching are less than consistent.

Baste to keep the layers in place, especially if the slot seam is used on a curved seamline. Shifting will throw off your carefully placed grain lines and result in unwelcome drag lines. Watch for seam allowance show-through when you press the seam—you may have to use paper strips to soften the effect. Visible seam allowances will spoil the effect of the clean lines of the slot and the carefully placed topstitching. Experiment with different types of thread— you may like the look of buttonhole twist. Your stitching will be more pronounced if you use a larger-than-usual stitch size.

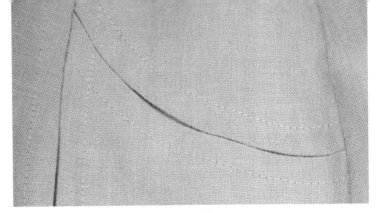

This curved faced slot seam incorporates a pocket.

Topstitched open seam

The topstitched open seam is an attractive variation of a welt seam in which the seam allowances are sewn toward the right side of the fashion fabric (as they are in the first step of a French seam), pressed open, and topstitched in place with the raw edges turned under. It's especially effective if there is a difference in texture, color, or weave between the right and wrong sides of the fabric. In addition to its decorative impact, it makes a clean finish for unlined garments.

Make samples to tell you how much extra seam allowance is needed; you'll probably want to add to the standard seam allowance, to make the seam treatment more noticeable. Samples will also tell you where to place the topstitching and which thread type and stitch size to use.

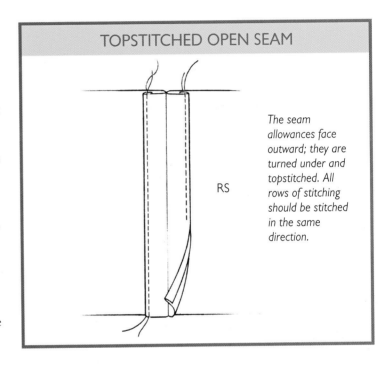

TOPSTITCHED OPEN SEAM

RS

The seam allowances face outward; they are turned under and topstitched. All rows of stitching should be stitched in the same direction.

Braced seam

Sometimes a strip of fabric is placed along the inside of a seamline and stitched in place—the result is a reinforced welt seam. But the fabric strip can also be placed on the outside, creating a braced seam. Apart from reinforcing the seam, the strip can be a striking fashion detail. This seam is sewn with wrong sides together, with the seam allowances on the right side of the fabric. In a braced seam, the fabric strip conceals the seam allowances (see the drawing on p. 64).

The strip, which is almost always cut on the bias, can be incorporated into the seamline on one side and then stitched along the other side, or it can overlay the seamline, centered above it. Cutting the strip on the bias allows it to follow curved seamlines, which this seam does a wonderful job of accentuating. The bias strip should be basted in place before stitching. Pins alone are insufficient. Also, the bias will shift with the weight of your presser foot, and pins tend to distort the bias in the area in which they're placed. Do all sewing in the same direction.

Topstitching accentuates this raised waistband and its open seam.

BRACED SEAM

RS

Often covered with a bias strip, a braced seam highlights curves. It's critical to stitch in the same direction. Basting the bias strip in place is a good idea, too.

Welt seam

Welt seams are defined by a single or double row of stitching, parallel to the seamline. If the seam allowances are pressed to one side (you may have to grade them), then a single row of stitching is applied; if the seam allowances are pressed open, then two rows of stitching are applied. Be sure to stitch all rows of topstitching in the same direction, and consider the use of an underlay (on the bias for the sake of flexibility) to add further strength.

Piped seam

In addition to being used around an edge (the neckline or armholes, for example), piping can be inserted into a seam. After making the piping, baste it into place, then stitch the seam. If you baste the piping carefully in place first, you'll need only a single row of machine stitching to sew the seam and encase the piping. An extra row of machine stitching will overly tighten the seam and may cause puckering.

SEAM FINISHES

Unless taken care of in the seam (as is the case with a French seam or a flat-fell seam, which automatically hides raw edges), seam allowances need to be finished to prevent unraveling. As you weigh your options for a seam finish, you'll ask yourself a number of questions:

- *What does the fabric suggest?*
- *What wear and tear will it be subjected to?*
- *How will the garment be cleaned?*
- *Does the fabric look as if it will need a great deal of control, or will it be well behaved?*
- *Is fraying a problem?*
- *What seam finishes do I like to do?*
- *What will be the finish's effect on the right side of the garment?*

Your answers to these questions will guide you in your choice, and the same garment will quite likely incorporate more than one type of seam finish. Seams often need to be finished after they've been stitched. Apart from pressing, they may need to be trimmed, graded, clipped, and notched before further treatment. When there is more than one layer of fabric in the seam allowances, stagger the clips so they don't fall on top of one another.

I like to leave seam allowances as wide as possible in areas that may one day need adjustment—side seams of skirts and trousers, for example. Moreover, a seam allowance that is too narrow, apart from running the risk of raveling, can create a short, hard ridge, especially if the fabric is thick or bulky; there isn't enough weight in the seam allowances to encourage them to lie flat.

If the fabric is handwoven or has the appearance of being handwoven, it is a candidate for careful control of raw edges. Even if a particularly ravelly fabric is covered with a lining, be sure you've taken care of the hidden raw edges.

Long seams, as in trousers, are more uniformly trimmed if cut with the layers together before the seam is pressed open, but overhandling will cause a loosely woven fabric to ravel, and even the slight preparation needed to ready it for an edge treatment will compromise the result. It's best to wait to trim the seam until just before finishing the edge.

It's sometimes easier to finish raw edges before stitching garment sections together (on long skirt seams, for example). Don't hesitate to put a catchstitch where necessary to hold seam allowances in place (provided there's an underlayer to attach them to). Sometimes a few well-placed hand stitches are the only way to make layers flat.

Although a serged edge is quick and easy to do, not to mention sturdy, there is an array of other choices, some of which add visual

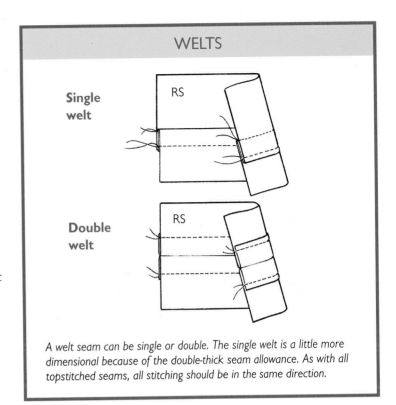

WELTS

Single welt

Double welt

A welt seam can be single or double. The single welt is a little more dimensional because of the double-thick seam allowance. As with all topstitched seams, all stitching should be in the same direction.

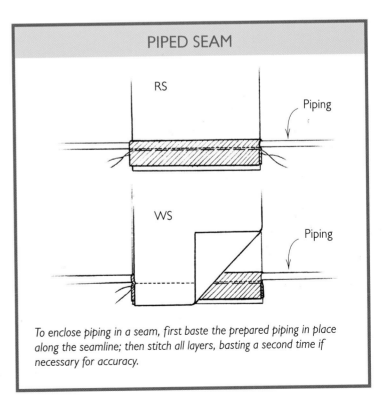

PIPED SEAM

To enclose piping in a seam, first baste the prepared piping in place along the seamline; then stitch all layers, basting a second time if necessary for accuracy.

ZIGZAG, FOLD, AND STITCH

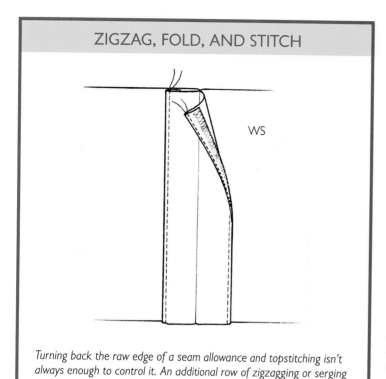

WS

Turning back the raw edge of a seam allowance and topstitching isn't always enough to control it. An additional row of zigzagging or serging guarantees control.

HAND OVERCASTING

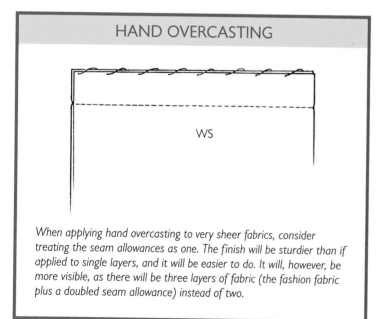

WS

When applying hand overcasting to very sheer fabrics, consider treating the seam allowances as one. The finish will be sturdier than if applied to single layers, and it will be easier to do. It will, however, be more visible, as there will be three layers of fabric (the fashion fabric plus a doubled seam allowance) instead of two.

appeal along with finishing off a raw edge. The approaches that follow all work well with cotton and linen.

Zigzag, fold, and stitch

This particular seam finish takes a little more time than a simple zigzag, but it's well worth the effort. A simple zigzag can look unruly and isn't always sturdy enough to control raveling in a loosely woven fabric. Even a turned and stitched seam, while clean looking, sometimes isn't enough to prevent raveling either. However, a combination of the two is effective, durable, and attractive.

This seam finish works best with relatively straight seams, but if you are using it on an off-grain edge, be sure to work from the wider end to the narrower end to control the grain better. Be sure you've allowed adequate width in the seam allowance for the trimming, zigzagging, and folding—an edge that is too narrow will be difficult to manipulate and stitch evenly.

Hand overcasting

There are times when a gentle, modest seam finish is needed—with a transparent fabric perhaps, or with a softly delicate fabric whose seam allowance would be marred by too heavy a treatment. A hand-overcast seam is the answer. Sturdy yet unobtrusive, it quietly gets the job done.

Sometimes the action of hand overcasting causes the thread to twist and kink. The problem may be the thread you're using, or it may be the action you take to sew the stitch. Either way, this tendency can be overcome by spinning the needle slightly with each stitch—a quarter turn or so in a counterclockwise direction if you're right-handed. It's easy to do and will soon become second nature. I find it easiest to twist the needle as I regrab it, just after it has passed through the fabric.

Hand overcasting works well with delicate fabrics such as voile, lawn, and handkerchief linen. Consider overcasting the seam allowances together, if a single layer is too sheer to control, but don't pull the stitches too tight or you'll lose the flat effect you're after. Be sure your thread is sufficiently long, so you don't run out mid-seam. It is difficult to rethread unobtrusively.

Hong Kong finish

A Hong Kong finish is in many ways an ideal seam finish—it's attractive, clean, and easy to control, and it works with a variety of fabric weights and textures and encourages seam allowances to lie flat. Begin by cutting strips of bias-cut fabric. Silk works well, as do rayon lining fabrics. Trim the seam allowance evenly, then apply the bias strip along its edge. Press the bias toward the outside edge, fold along the edge of the seam allowance, and stitch in the ditch. Be careful not to distort the bias; frequent pinning will help control placement.

Hong Kong lining

A clever way to line and finish edges at the same time is with a variation of the Hong Kong finish called a Hong Kong lining. Each garment section is in effect pre-lined, and its edges are finished off before the sections themselves are joined. It works well with straight seams and slightly curved seams, but not with anything dramatically curved.

Trim the seam allowance of the fashion fabric to the desired finished width. You'll need to cut the lining wider, though, because it needs extra width to wrap around and encase the edge of the seam allowance. Make the lining ½ in. wider than the edge to be finished—¼ in. for the visible part of the trim and ¼ in. to fold under to enclose the lining's raw edge. Make a paper or fabric sample if the concept confuses you, and you'll see the logic of it.

HONG KONG FINISH

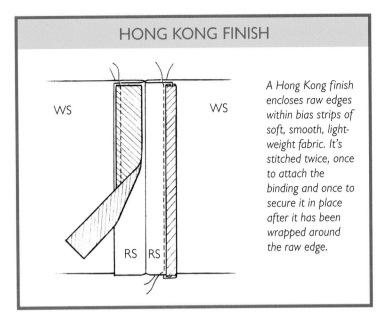

WS

WS

RS

RS

A Hong Kong finish encloses raw edges within bias strips of soft, smooth, lightweight fabric. It's stitched twice, once to attach the binding and once to secure it in place after it has been wrapped around the raw edge.

HONG KONG LINING

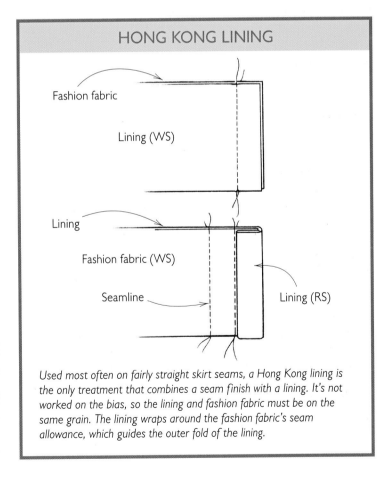

Fashion fabric

Lining (WS)

Lining

Fashion fabric (WS)

Seamline

Lining (RS)

Used most often on fairly straight skirt seams, a Hong Kong lining is the only treatment that combines a seam finish with a lining. It's not worked on the bias, so the lining and fashion fabric must be on the same grain. The lining wraps around the fashion fabric's seam allowance, which guides the outer fold of the lining.

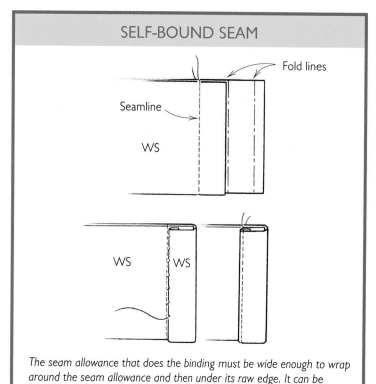

SELF-BOUND SEAM

Fold lines

Seamline

WS

WS   WS

The seam allowance that does the binding must be wide enough to wrap around the seam allowance and then under its raw edge. It can be finished by hand (for a softer result) or by machine (for a stiffer result).

Zigzagging and serging

Although not always very satisfactory on the lightest-weight fabrics (consider flat-fell seams, French seams, or hand overcasting instead), zigzagging and serging are suitable, hard-wearing seam finishes for medium-weight and heavyweight cottons and linens. One of the aims of these types of seam finishes is to be unobtrusive, so be careful that the stitches—and the amount of thread they contain—don't form a ridge that's noticeable on the right side of the garment.

Self-bound seam

For a self-bound seam, you'll need to leave an adequate seam allowance on the edge that will do the wrapping—at least three times the final width. Accuracy is critical, especially if the fabrics are at all transparent (e.g., voile, organdy, handkerchief linen). The wrapped seam allowance can be machine-stitched—which will add bulk by adding a row of machine stitching— or hand-stitched with a fell stitch or a slipstitch.

WAISTBANDS

Ask yourself the following questions before deciding upon what sort of waistline treatment is best for your skirt or trousers. How do you want the waistband to look, and how do you want it to feel? Will something tuck into it, and if so, how thick will that something be? Does the wearer prefer tight or loose waistbands? Is there apt to be a lot of strain on the waistband? If so, the sturdier the better. What inner stiffening will the waistband need? Is the waistband built up (i.e., does it extend considerably above the waist)? If so, it will require something special in the way of inner strengthening; it may benefit from boning. Would a waistline facing (a contour waistband or a grosgrain facing) be a flattering choice, as it lengthens the torso? Will the waistband fasten at the side, the back, or the front? How

Sew the lining and the fashion fabric, right sides together, matching their raw edges. Flip to the right side, and you'll find the lining falls into place, the raw edges of the seam allowances serving as a guide. Press the lining in place, pin carefully, and do a final row of machine stitching in the ditch, 1/4 in. in from the outside edge. Of course, you'll need to align the fashion fabric and the lining along the seamlines carefully before joining garment sections together. Hand basting will keep the layers in place.

The Hong Kong lining requires scrupulous accuracy with both seam allowance width and grain, or puckering, drag lines, and uneven (and unattractive) edges will result. Be careful of shifting. You'll probably be working with fabrics of very different weights—a heavy, textured linen with a lightweight crepe de Chine lining, for example—so be on the lookout for slipping.

much of an underlap needs to be allowed for a hook and eye and an extra snap to hold the underlap in place? Is the garment likely to be worn with a belt? If so, consider the belt's width and placement of belt carriers.

Begin by determining the exact waistline placement; it may be lower in the front than in the back, or vice versa. Keep in mind that from side to side, the front waistline measurement is almost always larger than the back waistline measurement.

Waistline treatments vary from minimal to heavily reinforced. Some sort of inner support, or strengthening, is necessary, though. The waist is the center of much movement—twisting, turning, and bending—as well as perspiring, all of which put a strain on the fabric and will undermine its appearance and comfort if the inner structure is less than adequate. Waistbands can be strengthened in a number of ways. Interfacing can support the fashion fabric of a standard waistband, a sturdy contoured facing will help support the waist area, or boning and heavy support can be added to a built-up waistband.

Before applying the waistband, carefully assess your garment's fit; make sure the trousers or skirt sits comfortably on the hips. Check it while you're standing up and while you're sitting down. If it's too tight around the hips, horizontal wrinkles will form, and it will ride up toward the waist. The garment will lose its charm and will be uncomfortable to wear.

I always put a line of staystitching directly on the waistline to mark it clearly. The staystitching also makes it easy for me to measure accurately and allows me to ease any areas that need to be adjusted (by carefully pulling the staystitches), regardless of what the waist treatment will be. Although cotton and linen can't be steamed and shaped like wool, a certain

CLIPPING THE WAISTLINE SEAM ALLOWANCE

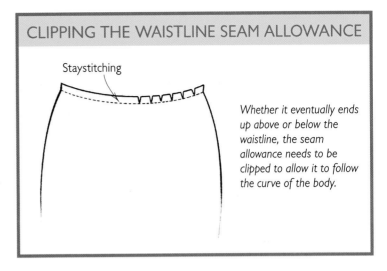

Staystitching

Whether it eventually ends up above or below the waistline, the seam allowance needs to be clipped to allow it to follow the curve of the body.

amount of easing is possible. For example, linen and cotton can usually be eased enough to eliminate a shallow hip dart if that is the desired effect.

If the fashion fabric is at all ravelly along the top edge of the skirt or trousers (it's usually cut on the crosswise grain and tends to fray easily), stitch a quick row of zigzagging along the top edge to control it. Be sure the seam allowances don't get flipped in the wrong direction as you stitch.

Once the staystitching has been applied, clip the waistline seam allowance. Skirt and trouser pieces always narrow toward the waist and continue to do so above the waist, which isn't what the body itself does. Clip the waist seam allowance so it can open up, accommodating the body's spread above the waist. Don't trim the inner seam allowance on the waistband, though. Whether you use a regular waistband, a contour waist facing, or a grosgrain facing, if you clip it a hard ridge will form. A little grading can be done, but be careful not to do too much. The strength the seam allowances give is more important than paring them down to reduce bulk.

Regular waistbands

A standard waistband is one in which a piece of fabric, usually reinforced in some way, anchors the garment. Its base rests along the actual waistline. You will need something inside the waistband to keep it from collapsing; I like to use a piece of preshrunk, 1-in.-wide grosgrain ribbon. It shouldn't be overly tight because it's an inner layer and there will be fashion fabric between it and the real waist, as well as thickness from anything that might be tucked in at the waist.

Remember to allow for a discrepancy of at least ½ in. between the waist measurement of the front of the figure and the back of the figure, even on the slimmest of bodies. Mark the grosgrain's center front, center back, and sides. Later, you will use these markings to line up the grosgrain accurately along the garment's waistline.

The waistband itself can be cut on the crosswise or the lengthwise grain. The crosswise grain has a little stretch to it, while the lengthwise grain will be more stable. If the waistband is placed along the selvage, that edge can be the finished edge at the inside of the waistband. The edge can also be serged, zigzagged, turned under, or edged with a Hong Kong finish.

The waistband itself can also be faced with another fabric, with the pieces joined along the folded edge at the top. Some fabrics are rough along the waistline, and some are bulky; a lightweight facing on the inner waistband, in place of the fashion fabric, can add comfort and reduce bulk (see the drawing at left). A bias waistband is tempting for the sake of a soft curve around the waist, but it's very difficult to get the bias to stay exactly true, especially where two circumferences are concerned (the inner waistband measurement is slightly smaller than the outer waistband measurement). Also, the movement of the body places strain in an unbalanced way, skewing the bias.

After I'm happy with the fit of the garment and the placement of the waist, I staystitch the waistline. Then I baste my measured and marked grosgrain ribbon in place on the outside of the garment (see the photo at left). Next I stitch the fashion-fabric waistband (making sure I don't catch the grosgrain in my stitching), fold it over, and finish the edge by hand or machine. I leave enough extra fabric on one end to create an

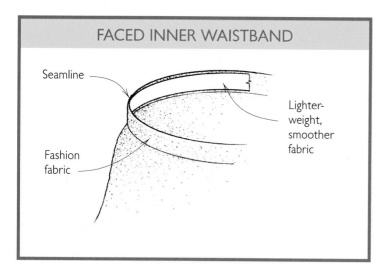

FACED INNER WAISTBAND

Seamline

Fashion fabric

Lighter-weight, smoother fabric

Grosgrain has been basted in place to the outside of the garment; it will be covered by the fashion-fabric waistband.

underlap, aligning it with the center of the opening (see the drawing at right). Extending the underlap rather than the overlap will give a cleaner-looking finish.

Built-up waistbands

The only real distinction between a built-up waistband and a regular waistband is the inner support that the built-up waistband requires. A built-up waistband can be striking, but its impact will be diminished if it's undermined by inadequate inner support. Experiment to gauge just how much inner structure you will need. Boning is one of the best methods. A properly boned waistband literally can't collapse. The boning can be applied to the facing of the waistband; the inner layers will camouflage its presence.

Contoured waistbands

Technically, a contoured waistband is a facing. Like a waistband, it functions as an anchor in the waist area and as a source of support for the attached garment. A contoured facing is probably the most comfortable of waistline treatments. It requires careful fitting to make it sit perfectly, right below the waistline and accurately contoured to rest on the flare of the hips. A separate facing pattern is easy to trace from the skirt or trouser pattern, once the fit has been established. Be sure to keep the grain lines identical.

Contoured facings can incorporate careful shaping below the waistline, precisely echoing figure variations and idiosyncrasies. They are comfortable and cool to wear. A lining can quickly and easily be attached to the bottom of the facing. If there is no lining or if the lining has been attached in the traditional manner at the waistline, the edge of the facing will need to be finished off. The edge can be serged, zigzagged,

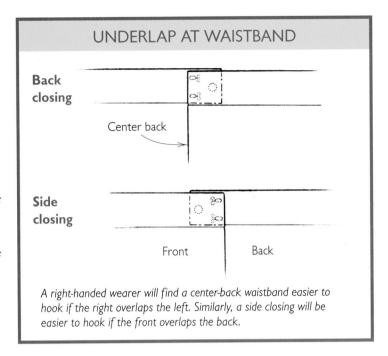

UNDERLAP AT WAISTBAND

Back closing

Center back

Side closing

Front   Back

A right-handed wearer will find a center-back waistband easier to hook if the right overlaps the left. Similarly, a side closing will be easier to hook if the front overlaps the back.

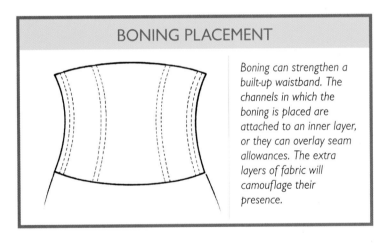

BONING PLACEMENT

Boning can strengthen a built-up waistband. The channels in which the boning is placed are attached to an inner layer, or they can overlay seam allowances. The extra layers of fabric will camouflage their presence.

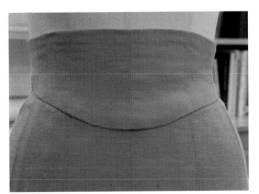

A wide built-up waistband is a focal point of this red linen skirt.

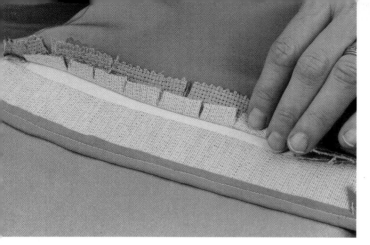
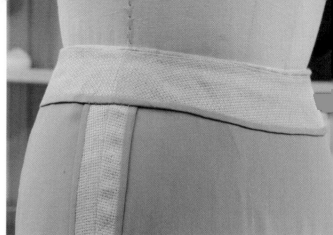

At left, stay tape applied inside a contoured waistband helps keep the waistband from stretching; the inside of the finished skirt is seen at right.

Shape grosgrain by steaming it, contouring it to the pattern.

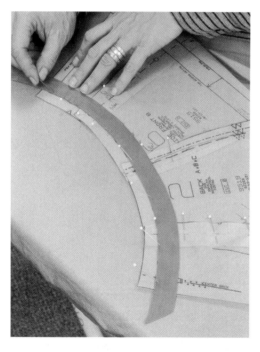

The actual waist measurement will be the smallest (e.g., 26 in.), the contour facing will be slightly larger (e.g., 26½ in.), and the garment will be larger still (e.g., 27 in.).

The facing can be interfaced with a fusible or a sew-in interfacing. It needs to be sturdy (but not stiff), it needs to stay flat, and its lower edge must be finished without creating a detectable ridge. To apply a contour facing, prepare the facing, including the finishing of its lower edge. Determine the waistline, and staystitch at the waistline. Apply stay tape to the waistline by hand or machine; otherwise, the waistline will grow (body heat and movement will stretch it). Stitch the facing, and clip the seam allowances of the facing and the garment. With the seam allowances carefully turned toward the facing, understitch the facing. Press the garment, favoring the facing so the seamline is toward the inside. Tack the facing to the garment as necessary (at side seams and darts). Use a hook and eye, or a tab with a button at the top of the zipper, for security. Be sure it isn't detectable by any pulling or strain on the underlayers.

faced with the interfacing, or trimmed with a Hong Kong finish. Be careful that the edge of the facing isn't detectable from the right side of the garment, whichever finish you choose.

Start by taking careful measurements of the body, the contour facing, and the garment. They all will have different circumferences.

If the garment seems a little loose, try feeding a band of elastic through the facing (between the facing and its sewn-in interfacing) or between the fashion fabric and the facing (if the facing's interfacing has been fused). Although the elastic won't be stretched, it will serve to anchor the facing and "snug it" onto the wearer's hips. (If the elastic were pulled too tight, it would cause the garment to creep up above the waist-line). Tack it in place as necessary.

Grosgrain waistbands

Grosgrain waistbands are quick and easy to apply. They are a simple variation of the contour facing, in which the facing is replaced by a shaped piece of grosgrain ribbon. It's not the sturdiest of waist treatments, but there are times when a lightweight waistband, free of bulk, is exactly what's needed.

You will first need to find the proper grosgrain. Real grosgrain (and the only one that can be shaped by steam) has tiny scallops along each edge. It's a little difficult to find (try tailoring supply houses). Unfortunately, the grosgrain at your local fabric store isn't the right kind. It has a woven edge that won't shrink and stretch the way you need it to, and it won't be sturdy enough to form a substantial facing.

Prepare the grosgrain by steaming it. It will shape easily as you stretch one edge and shrink the other. Line it up along the waist-line of the garment to get the correct shape, or refer back to the paper pattern. Be sure to incorporate in its width any changes you may have made in the fit.

To apply a grosgrain facing, first staystitch the waistline. Then serge or zigzag the raw edge. Hand- or machine-baste the prepared grosgrain into place, lining it up along the waistline. Extend it on either end of the opening. Both ends can be folded in, flush with the zipper opening, or one side can extend to form an underlap. Sew the grosgrain onto the seam allowance, ⅛ in. to ¼ in. below the staystitching. Clip the

Visible inside this completed grosgrain waistband are the staystitching, understitching, zigzagging to control the seam allowance, and, at right, one of a series of small tacks that will hold the waistband in place.

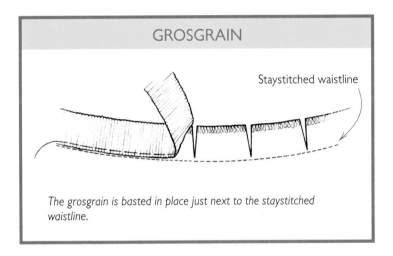

GROSGRAIN

Staystitched waistline

The grosgrain is basted in place just next to the staystitched waistline.

waistline seam allowance so it will be able to spread once it has been folded down into place. Fold the grosgrain into place and press. Secure the grosgrain at darts, seam-lines, and along the opening. If there is an underlap, use a hook and eye and a snap to hold it in place.

6 Inside the Garment

One of the things that lifts sewing above the ordinary is the use of inner structure and inner support. While not all garments need inner support, many benefit from carefully analyzed and carefully placed elements of inner structure, which can be extensive at times. Interfacing, underlining, staystitching, and stays are your tools that add inner structure and support. Once you become familiar with all that they can do for you, your sewing will become more rewarding. Your garments will look and feel better and wear longer, thanks to what's going on inside.

INTERFACINGS

Interfacing is a layer of fabric inserted between the fashion fabric and a facing. It's one of the most important tools a sewer has, for it lends support and structure, which can be subtle or pronounced, to specific areas of a garment. It reinforces, shapes, and stabilizes specific areas, controls stretching, adds body, supports the weight of the garment, and sets off details. If well chosen and carefully prepared and applied, it can do wonders for the integrity of a gar-

ment, whether in the small details of a collar or cuff or in its overall strength.

Obviously, some garments are perfectly successful without any interfacing at all. As often as not, cotton and linen garments are lightweight and easy to wear. Sometimes adequate support can come from the care with which you construct and fit the garment and from its facings, plackets, and turnbacks themselves. However, most garments benefit from at least some interfacing, and many couldn't survive without a generous amount of it. Common placements for interfacing include collars, cuffs, the shoulder area, buttonholes, pockets, waistbands, and hems. Sometimes entire garment sections are interfaced, especially if the fashion fabric is unstable or the garment is particularly weighty, or if considerable shaping is required of a fabric that isn't quite up to the task.

Picture your finished garment. Is it a sharply tailored suit, with its collar and pockets crisply defined? Or is it a gently flowing blouse, its collar and cuffs softly curving into place? The right interfacings can help achieve these looks, once a careful

Various fusibles were considered for this shifty basket-weave linen.

assessment of your needs points you in the right direction. Different parts of the garment often require different interfacings. What strengthens the shoulder area may be too strong for the collar. What stabilizes the waistband may be too stiff for the pockets. You may even decide your garment will work beautifully without any interfacing at all. Remember that the proper placement and choices of interfacing begin with assessment, followed by thorough experimentation with the possibilities. Interfacing can help your garment enormously, so your first job is to determine where your garment needs help.

Ask yourself some questions to determine where and what kind of interfacing you need. What parts of the garment need strengthening? Will the shoulder area be doing the major work of supporting the garment? Where do you want stiffness? On a dramatic collar? Where do you want soft shaping? On a gently draped neckline? Is the garment loose fitting and unlikely to bear much strain, or is it tight fitting and something in which the wearer will be active? Are the buttonholes and pockets more than decorative? Is it likely to be worn often, or is it a garment for formal occasions, worn carefully and subject to little wear and tear? Will it be hand-washed, machine-washed and machine-dried, or dry-cleaned?

The answers to such questions will play into your interfacing choices, choices that must be suited to each garment's unique

combination of fabrication, design, and use. There is no golden rule, no magic formula for interfacing choice and placement. The decision is yours, based first upon your careful assessment of your garment's needs, and then upon your thorough experimentation with the possibilities.

Interfacings fall into two main categories: sew-in and fusible. The quality, availability, and ease of use of fusibles make them the automatic first choice of many sewers, but don't overlook traditional sew-in interfacings. Although fusibles are widely popular, there is a subtlety to sew-in interfacing that you may prefer. I often feel the true nature of the fabric is better preserved with a sew-in interfacing than with a fusible one.

Whichever you choose, make samples using the fashion fabric with different interfacing possibilities. Then ask yourself the following questions: Has the surface, texture, or color of the fashion fabric changed? Do the fashion fabric and the interfacing have similar stretch? Have those qualities been maintained after joining the two? Manipulate the sample. Do you like the feel? Does the interfacing do enough? Or does it do too much? Does it change the nature of the fabric more than you'd like? Will some parts of the garment need firmer interfacing than others? Do you want the hand of the fabric to be crisp and stiff? Soft and flowing? Sturdy and firm? Interfacing can do all of these things, but ask yourself what it is you want. Will the interfacing change the fabric so much that its initial appeal will be lost? Is there a noticeable (and unwelcome) distinction, or even a ridge, between the area that's been interfaced and the area that hasn't been? Does the interfacing overpower the fashion fabric? Fold the fabric. Does it fold the way you'd like, or does it crease into a hard fold? Does it fold easily or reluctantly? If it's too stiff, your interfacing may be overpowering the fashion fabric. What is the effect of the interfacing when used on the straight of grain? On the bias? If you'll be making

Interfacing can be applied using the tissue pattern as a guide, especially if the garment section is irregularly shaped.

buttonholes—hand, machine, or bound—do a test. Are you happy with the result? Are your buttonholes adequately reinforced?

Use less interfacing rather than more, at least initially. You can always go back and add some if necessary. Be especially careful when choosing interfacing that will be used throughout a garment, and remember that fusibles are firmer once fused.

Your choice will have a huge effect on the garment's overall appearance, and you want that to be the right effect. There's no point in turning a soft cotton blouse into a piece of cardboard (which you could do, easily enough), nor is there any reason to have an undersupported jacket that would clearly benefit from a little inside structure in the right areas. Interfacing should enhance, rather than overpower or obscure the fabric's inherent charms and characteristics, unless you want it to.

Be sure you've interfaced any small areas that will bear strain, such as pocket edges, the area around a kick pleat, Vs, corners, tops of godets, gussets, and the fabric behind heavy buttons.

Consider placing interfacing on the bias in collars and cuffs. It will enhance their curves. Apply interfacing to the topside (outside) of collars and cuffs. This will lessen the possibility of seeing seam allowances, but be sure it isn't too stiff. Lightweight, or featherweight, interfacing applied to both sides of collars and cuffs is a solution worth considering. It has the advantage of stabilizing the garment sections identically so it will be easier to sew them together accurately. Interfacing is usually cut out of the seam allowance of a collar point; it can add too much bulk.

Consider strengthening a sew-in interfacing with a fusible. The fusible may be too stiff to be adhered directly to the fashion fabric, but it may be able to do its work by being attached to a sew-in interfacing or to an underlining. Attaching the interfacing to the underlining will eliminate bulk in the seam area. Since the underlining is caught in the seamline, the interfacing needn't be. Underlinings and interfacings can be quilted together; the rows of stitching will add body.

Sometimes the contrast in color of an interfacing is an asset. Red thread on red fashion fabric can be difficult to see, but red thread on beige interfacing is easy to see. If attaching a fusible to an unstable piece of fabric (an armhole facing, for example), use the tissue pattern as a template. Check the grain of the fashion fabric and the fusible against the tissue pattern and keep the pattern in place as you fuse (see the photo above).

Before actually applying any interfacing, sew-in or fusible, it has to be preshrunk. Obviously, it will eventually be treated the same as the fashion fabric, so the two have to be thoroughly compatible.

Fusible interfacing

Choices for fusibles include tricot (knit), weft-insertion (in which stabilizing threads are inserted crosswise into a tricot), warp-insertion (in which stabilizing threads are inserted lengthwise into a tricot), all bias, and non-stretch. Fusibles are available in a limited, but generally adequate range of colors (white, black, sometimes beige and gray). For a list of the most popular fusible interfacings, see the sidebar on p. 78. Fortu-

Interfacing is readily available at fabric stores. Here are some popular choices:

- **Armo-Weft.** A weft-insertion interfacing stable on the crosswise grain, yet flexible.

- **Easy Knit.** Tricot lightweight, with a crosswise stretch.

- **French Fuse.** Tricot lightweight, for soft body, with a crosswise stretch.

- **Fusi-Knit.** Tricot lightweight, for soft body, with a crosswise stretch.

- **Sheer D'light.** Featherweight and lightweight non-woven with crosswise stretch.

- **SofBrush.** Lightweight warp-insertion, with crosswise stretch.

- **Sofshape.** Nonwoven all bias.

- **Whisper Weft.** Weft-insertion; soft and stable, yet flexible.

nately, there is almost always more than one successful choice for interfacing, and since you'll be testing the possibilities before you use them on the fashion fabric, there's plenty of opportunity to choose wisely.

In general, wovens add strength and stability, and knits add flexibility and drape. But beyond those sweeping generalizations, there are endless shades of gray. Experimentation will yield clues as to the success of the match, so be sure to have plenty of extra fabric and interfacing on hand. Generally, sew-ins can be adequately assessed by draping the fashion fabric over them, but you'll need to make samples of fusibles.

Fusible interfacings will shrink if exposed to moisture and heat so, for optimum results, they should be soaked in hot water and then steamed just before fusing, as described below. Fold the interfacing and place it in hot tap water for at least 20 minutes, being careful not to disturb the resins

by agitating it. Then drain, and roll the fusible in a towel to remove most of the water. Hang it over a shower rod to dry, or, in the case of a fusible tricot, dry it flat.

Since fusibles can't be pressed to remove wrinkles, avoid wrinkles by carefully folding the fusible until you're ready to use it. I easily confuse fusible brand names, so I always write the name (and manufacturer) on one end of the piece and make sure I do my cutting from the other end.

Fusibles need to be affixed to the fashion fabric with a combination of moisture, pressure, and time. Prepare the fashion fabric by ironing it. This will remove any wrinkles, and it will warm up the fabric in preparation for fusing. Put the fusible in place, resin side down. You've taken care of some of the shrinkage by soaking it in hot water, but it will further benefit from being steamed. Steam it just before you fuse it, by holding the iron an inch or so above it, keeping it in place for about 5 seconds. Move the iron until you've steamed the entire piece.

Fuse the interfacing by pressing on it. You are squeezing the resins down into the fabric, so firm pressure is critical. (You may want to lower your ironing board; you'll be able to use more of your body weight.) Unless your iron produces a steady, generous amount of steam, use a moist pressing cloth. The pressing cloth will also lessen the chance of the fusible's resins seeping into your iron's sole plate. Count to 10— slowly—without moving your iron, then move to the next section, overlapping slightly.

When you have finished, allow the fabrics to cool before you move them or you'll destabilize them. Finally, turn the fused fabric over and repeat the process, using a pressing cloth to prevent shine. Check that the fusible is well adhered to the fashion fabric, especially at the edges and corners, and make sure that there are no bubbles or show-through from the resins. You don't want a fusible interfacing to overhang the edge of the piece of fabric it's interfacing. If it extends beyond the edge of the fashion fabric, it may attach itself somewhere to the inside of the garment, causing unwelcome pulling.

Sew-in interfacing

Choices for woven sew-ins include silk organza (soft and crisp), cotton batiste (soft and strong in a gentle way), muslin (sturdy), taffeta (lightweight but firm), self-fabric (the most compatible of all if it's not too bulky), and non-woven sew-ins. If the color of the interfacing is a factor, natural-fiber sew-ins can be dyed. Non-woven sew-ins are also available.

For sew-in interfacing, machine-wash and dry the interfacing if the fashion fabric will be treated that way. If the garment will be dry-cleaned, wash the interfacing by hand and line dry.

Sew-ins are joined to the fashion fabric along seamlines. They can be machine-basted in place, but basting them in by hand will give more accurate results and eliminate shifting

UNDERLININGS

Underlining is a layer of fabric (and in certain cases, even more than one layer) that is applied to an individual garment section. After the two have been joined, they are treated as one. While interfacing is generally applied to a specific area of a garment, with its primary effect on shape and structure, underlining is applied directly to the fashion fabric, and it is upon the fashion fabric that its effects are felt. If well chosen, its presence is undetectable to the wearer. To the sewer, however, its presence can be invaluable.

You may love a fabric's color, texture, and drape, but it may be lacking the inner strength needed for it to do what you want or need it to do. Underlining can transform a too-light fabric into a fabric of just the right weight. But apart from its primary role, its effect on the fabric, there are lots of smaller, and very important, ways in which it also lends help. It camouflages seam allowances, it hides hand-sewing stitches (they go onto the underlining, not the fashion fabric), it can help adjust the color of the fashion fabric, it reduces wrinkling, and it absorbs perspiration. The underlining can be marked without marring the fashion fabric, it adds modesty to a sheer fabric, it can improve the drape of a fabric, and it can serve as a base for interfacing.

Linens and cottons aren't always candidates for underlining, especially when used for lightweight, freely moving garments. But if they're used for a more structured garment, then consider underlining. It may just add that little bit of overall support that your fabric needs to firm it up, to give it "oomph."

Underlinings are almost always sewn in. On a particularly loosely woven or unstable fabric, a fusible could serve as an underlining but it might change the basic nature of the fabric too much. It's backing (another name for underlining, in fact) and underlying support you're after, with the fabric maintaining its "hand" and its natural movement. Silk organza is a wonderful underlining. Lightweight and crisp, it adds just a touch of firmness. Cotton batiste is another favorite that lends softer support. Muslin is also a possibility for firmer support. Sometimes garments are self-underlined, guaranteeing identical behavior and care. Even though it may be lightweight and soft, an underlining needs to be firmly woven.

Before joining the underlining to the fashion fabric, first mark the underlining (checking to make sure marks won't show through to the fashion fabric if you're using tracing paper). Then pin the layers together in the seam allowances, carefully lining up the grainlines on each layer. Then flip the

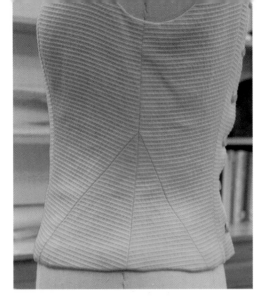

This Valentino ottoman vest has a silk organza underlining that helps fortify and shape the fabric. It also provides a base for hand stitches.

The silk organza doubles the fashion fabric. Once joined, the two layers are treated as one.

garment section so the fashion fabric is right side up and smooth it out. The fashion fabric must be taut. Adjust the pins and flip the section back over to baste the layers together. The underlining may appear slightly baggy, which is fine; it's more important that the outer layer—the fashion fabric—be taut.

The layers can be joined by hand or machine. Joining them by hand usually guarantees greater accuracy. Stitch each edge, following the stitching lines, going all the way to the end of each before breaking the thread and starting on the next edge (see the top drawing on the facing page).

You can take a shortcut, if you're hand-basting, by turning the corner with your thread (see the bottom drawing on the facing page), but be sure you go all the way to the end of each edge before changing directions. Your basting stitches can be placed just outside the stitching line. If they are too far from the stitching line, the layers may shift when it comes time to join the garment sections. I like to hand-baste on the stitching line, for the sake of accuracy, but it does mean I have to do lots of tedious basting-stitch removal. Use a single strand of silk thread, if you can find it, for your basting; it will pull out more easily than other types of thread. If you're working on light-colored fabrics, avoid basting with dark thread. Although it will be easier on your eyes, the color may bleed, and at the very least, small fibers will rub off, and they'll be impossible to remove.

Basted hemlines will in all likelihood have to be adjusted later. The weight of the fashion fabric, once it's hanging vertically rather than being worked on on a flat surface, will cause slight shifts in the layers. It's easy to realign them before you hem.

By the time you've joined the layers, not only will the underlining be mounted to the fashion fabric, but your seamlines will also be clearly marked by your basting threads, ensuring accuracy as you construct your garment.

FACINGS

A facing is a piece of fabric, usually separate from the garment, that both finishes raw edges and strengthens them and the surrounding area. Mirroring the shape of what they face, they're typically found at necklines and armholes. Sleeves and hems are sometimes faced as well. The seamlines to which facings are sewn are often curved, at least in part. A facing can be visible or invisible, made from the fashion fabric or a contrasting fabric. Although it can be a design element, its primary purpose is structural.

Consider the neckline, for example. It not only is a visual focal point but also has structural importance. Most garments hang from the shoulders, so ask yourself what will give definition, structurally and stylistically, to the neckline and other areas that need to be faced. If you choose to replace facings with bias binding, be sure you haven't eliminated critical support that the garment needs. Compensate by strengthening, or adding, interfacing or underlining.

Regular facings

Applying facings in cotton and linen garments is a straightforward process. Begin by copying any changes that have been made at the garment's edges onto the facing pattern, taking care to match grainlines accurately. Grain must be exactly the same on the garment and its facings. The layers need to move in concert and can do so only if their grains are exactly the same. Use a French curve to smooth out any alterations and a tracing wheel to trace new seamlines. If the changes you've made are significant, you may need to draw a new pattern piece.

Grade the seam allowances, leaving the seam allowance next to the outside of the garment the longest. After pressing and clipping the seam allowances, understitch, making sure to catch all seam allowances in the stitching. As you stitch, spread the fabric to either side of the needle with your hands, to control shifting.

The edge of the facing needs to be finished. Among the choices for finishing the edge are pinking, or stitching and pinking. These methods are quick, but not very sturdy. Serging or zigzagging is also a quick method, but be wary of applying too much thread to the edge. It could show through on the right side. You can face the facing

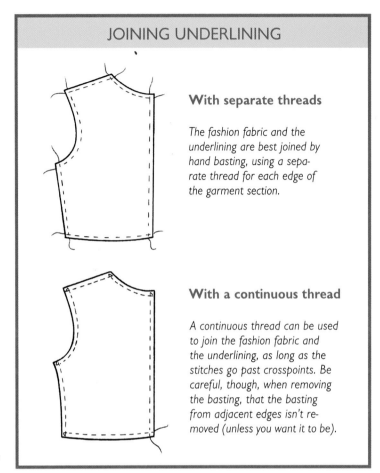

JOINING UNDERLINING

With separate threads

The fashion fabric and the underlining are best joined by hand basting, using a separate thread for each edge of the garment section.

With a continuous thread

A continuous thread can be used to join the fashion fabric and the underlining, as long as the stitches go past crosspoints. Be careful, though, when removing the basting, that the basting from adjacent edges isn't removed (unless you want it to be).

with interfacing (see the sidebar on p. 82), which gives you a clean edge. A Hong Kong finish (see p. 67) is an elegant treatment; just be sure it doesn't leave a detectable ridge. Rayon linings, silk chiffon, and voile are all possibilities for the binding fabric used in a Hong Kong finish.

Facings can be held in place by tacking them at seamlines, darts, and the opening. A neck facing can also be stitched along the shoulder, in the seamline, but be sure the stitching doesn't create a noticeable indentation. It may be better simply to tack it.

The hems of sleeves and skirts can also be faced. A bias facing encourages the edge to curve gracefully. The facing needs to be cut

Interfacing is often applied to facings, and the treatment of the non-sewn edge is always a concern. The edge could be serged, it could be pinked, it could be zigzagged; but there's another option: facing the facing. It's a technique that works with both sew-ins and fusibles. Sew the right sides of the interfacing and the fashion fabric together along the outside edge. Trim, clip, and turn so that the wrong sides are together. Press (see the photo at right); if the facing is a fusible, you'll have to press carefully, with the layers correctly placed, because your pressing will also fuse them. The outside edges will now be neatly finished, and little bulk will have been added. ■

Facings can be faced with fusible interfacing.

incrementally smaller than the garment. Its circumference is, after all, smaller, and it needn't be understitched.

Narrow bias facings

A narrow bias strip can function as a facing. It will need topstitching to hold it in place, unless there is a lining or underlining onto which it can be stitched. To apply, first stabilize the area by staystitching the garment along the edges to be faced. Check the placement of the staystitching for symmetry before applying the bias strip. Prepare a bias strip with two folded edges. Align one fold line along the stitching line and pin (or baste) carefully. Take care that the bias doesn't stretch as it's being stitched. Stitch just inside (toward the garment) the staystitching line, or the staystitches may be visible when the facing is turned. Overlap the bias at the join, folding the raw edge of the topmost strip under. Trim and clip the seam allowance of the garment. Press the facing toward the edge of the garment, then fold it in place, favoring it so that the seamline is slightly inside the folded edge.

The facing needs to be carefully topstitched; the stitching will be visible, after all. Check thread, stitch length, placement, and tension. You may prefer two rows of stitching—one close to the fold line, the second along the far edge of the facing. Use plenty of pins to prevent shifting, and if you do two rows of stitching, stitch them in the same direction. Don't overlap the stitching, and hide the thread tails inside the garment.

If the garment is lined, the bias facing can be hand-stitched (with a fell stitch or a slipstitch) to the lining. Although it won't have the security that topstitching provides, it can be stitched invisibly.

Self-facings

Perhaps the simplest facing of all is one in which the seam allowance is turned back. There are two prerequisites, though. There needs to be something to secure the facing to, and the seam allowance needs to be covered up. Otherwise, it really wouldn't be a very attractive finish.

Your first step is to make sure that the turn-back is of sufficient width—at a neck edge, 1 in. or 1½ in. is workable, and ¾ in. is sufficient at armholes. To apply, reinforce and define the fold line with a row of staystitching. Fold over, clipping as necessary for the edge to lie flat and smooth, favoring it to the inside (see the bottom drawing at right). Frequent, shallow clips are better than fewer, deeper clips. Although the seam allowance can be catchstitched to an inner layer, it will sometimes stay in place by itself; the lining will help keep it in place (see the top photo on p. 84).

The seam allowance will need to be covered with a lining. Prepare the lining by staystitching its seamline, clipping and turning the seam allowance so the staystitching won't be visible, and stitching it in place with a fell stitch, just inside the fold line. Machine understitching isn't possible, as the seam allowance is already stitched in place, but understitching can be applied by hand, using a prick stitch, running it through all layers except the fashion fabric. It's a secure, elegant finish—a little extra work, but worth the effort. It gives a lovely definition to the garment's edges.

Using the lining as a facing

It's always a challenge to face the neckline and armholes of an unlined bodice without any inner layers. Traditional facings often don't behave, and if they are tacked anywhere other than seamlines and darts, the stitches are obvious. If the facings are tacked only there, pulling can occur and the unruly facings can show. Necklines and armholes can be bound with bias binding, but this doesn't offer much stability. After all, it's only the edge that's being treated. Edges can be faced with a narrow bias strip, which is then topstitched in place, but topstitching may not be desirable. There is a way, however, to face both the neckline and armholes with the bodice lining. Although the method is a little tricky, it's an alternative worth considering. This method requires careful cutting and accurate marking, as the two layers must be mirror images. There mustn't be any pulling or bagging once the edges are turned (see the bottom photo on p. 84). That is only possible if the garment sections have been prepared and marked with total accuracy.

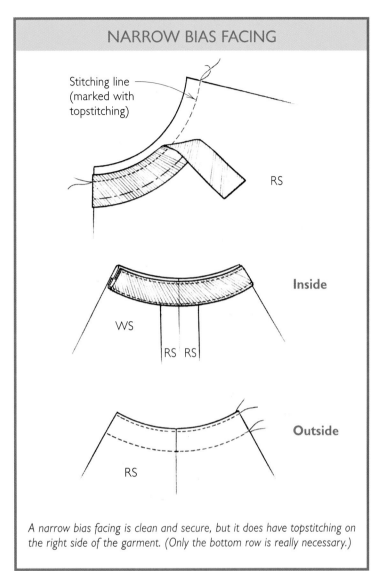

NARROW BIAS FACING

Stitching line (marked with topstitching)

RS

Inside

WS

RS   RS

Outside

RS

A narrow bias facing is clean and secure, but it does have topstitching on the right side of the garment. (Only the bottom row is really necessary.)

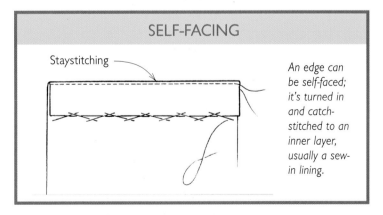

SELF-FACING

Staystitching

An edge can be self-faced; it's turned in and catch-stitched to an inner layer, usually a sew-in lining.

The seam allowance is pressed inward; the carefully matched lining will be fell-stitched in place, controlling the edge.

In this lightweight cotton bodice, the lining doubles as an effective facing.

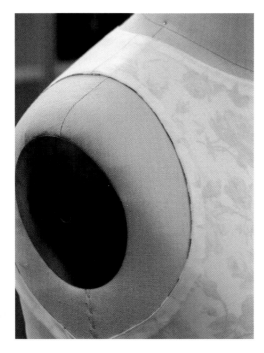

To apply, sew and press open the shoulder seams of each layer, leaving the side seams unstitched. Join the layers, right sides together, and stitch the neckline and the armholes. Trim the seam allowances and clip, staggering the clips. Do as much pressing as you can, with the seam allowances turned toward the facing. Pull the lining through to the right side, threading it through the shoulder seams (see the top drawing on the facing page). Understitch as far as possible. Sew the side seams. The slipperier and thinner the lining, the easier it will be to pull through at the shoulders.

If the shoulder seams are at all narrow, it's difficult, if not impossible, to understitch entirely around each edge. In all likelihood, you will have to sew each edge from two different directions, or at least in two segments. A shoulder seam of 2 in. or so should allow you, with careful manipulation and trimming, to understitch all edges.

When sewing the side seams, sew them each in two segments so you'll avoid stitching the seam allowance at the underarm (see the middle drawing on the facing page). This will enable you to get a smooth curve at the base of the sleeve. Incorporating the seam allowances in the seam would pull it in one direction or the other, and the base of the underarm seam would form a V rather than curve. Finish the armhole by placing the final length of understitching along the lower edge. Hide thread tails inside.

Inserting piping into a facing

Piping can be applied to a garment edge, adding visual definition and structural reinforcement. In order to be effective, though, it has to be prepared and applied with care. Begin by cutting absolutely true bias, filled with cording of the proper circumference. (Try mousetail or rattail; they're smoother than cable cord, whose twisted threads are sometimes visible through lightweight cotton and linen piping.) Hand-baste the edge of the bias strips together before machine-stitching, in order to eliminate any shifting (see the bottom drawing on the facing page). Experiment to get the best zipper-foot placement; the cord must be securely held inside the piping, but it mustn't be too tight, or it will lose its flexibility.

To apply, baste the prepared piping into place. Machine-stitch the piping. Attach a facing by machine or by hand (if by hand, fell-stitch it in place, using small stitches to eliminate gaps between stitches).

If puckering is a problem, consider eliminating a row of machine stitching by attaching the piping first by hand, and only by machine when the facing is sewn in place. Increasing the stitch size may help reduce puckering, too. The lining can be sewn in place by machine or by hand. Thanks to the presence of the piping, the folded edge of the lining is recessed from the finished edge and will be hidden by the piping.

It's relatively easy to apply piping to an outer corner as long as it has been clipped right at the corner and carefully stitched. An inner corner (if close to, or tighter than, a right angle) is impossible without some sort of a fold creeping into the piping. Although piping can accommodate quite a curve, it cannot turn a corner without forming a fold. An alternative is to form a corner with overlapping pieces of piping. First, prepare the corner of the garment with small reinforcing stitches, and clip into the corner. Then sew two pieces of piping together, angling them to match the angle of the corner on the garment. Finally, sew on the stitched-together piping in two steps. With the piping on the bottom, sew one side of the corner, then the other (see the photo on p. 86).

LININGS

Although linings are not always used in linen and cotton garments, sometimes a lightweight lining is worth considering. It offers a number of advantages. A lining protects the inside of the garment from wear, tear, and perspiration, it helps the garment slide on and off easily (especially a jacket), and it adds a layer of modesty. It can serve as a facing and can help camouflage the work behind the scenes. It lessens wrinkling, reduces stretch in the seat and knees of a garment, eliminates the need for some inside finishing, and can add a degree of structure.

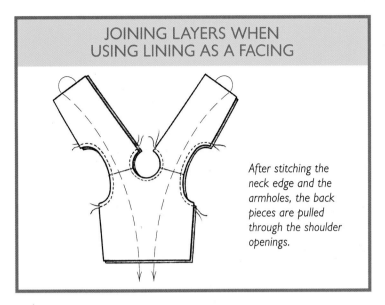

JOINING LAYERS WHEN USING LINING AS A FACING

After stitching the neck edge and the armholes, the back pieces are pulled through the shoulder openings.

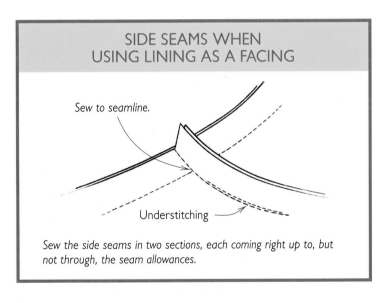

SIDE SEAMS WHEN USING LINING AS A FACING

Sew to seamline.

Understitching

Sew the side seams in two sections, each coming right up to, but not through, the seam allowances.

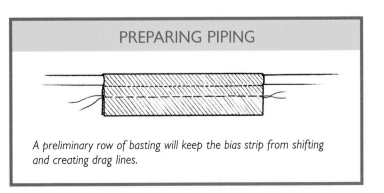

PREPARING PIPING

A preliminary row of basting will keep the bias strip from shifting and creating drag lines.

On corners too sharp for the piping to turn smoothly, short sections can be sewn separately, making the corners stylish and well defined.

the garment pattern pieces, be sure to make the same adjustments to the lining. If the lining is a print, be sure the designs don't show through the fashion fabric. Linen and cotton garments can be thin, without the inner layers that we're accustomed to in heavier lined garments. You may, though, like the effect of the lining peeking out along the facing and armholes. Consider using the lining fabric to line pockets and/or for facings. Finely woven cotton is a sturdy yet lightweight choice. If the garment's neck and armholes will be finished with a bias binding (either as a visible trim or as a topstitched facing), the lining can be used almost as an underlining. Baste the layers together at the neck and armholes before applying the bias binding. Use a jump pleat (a horizontal fold of fabric that allows movement) at jacket hems, skirt hems, and sleeve hems.

Skirt and trouser linings

Consider converting the darts in the lining of a skirt or trousers into small pleats. They will give you more wearing ease. Fold them in the opposite direction and press them flat to reduce bulk. Insert the lining, carefully matching up seams, darts, and pleats. Hand- or machine-baste the layers together at the waistline before adding the waistband. Fold the seam allowances of the lining inward along the zipper (or other closure). Fell-stitch the lining in place.

Linings of gathered or pleated skirts can be pared down to reduce bulk (change gathers to pleats, make pleats less deep) as long as sufficient walking ease remains. If hanging free at the hemline, the lining should be at least 1 in. shorter than the skirt or trouser hem. Use French tacks to hold the lining in place (see the drawing on the facing page). However, on a lined, circular skirt, French-tacking the fashion fabric and the lining would impede the natural flow of the garment; there will be sufficient weight in

A number of fabrics work well as linings for cotton and linen garments. Beyond silk linings (China silk and crepe de Chine, for garments that will be dry-cleaned), rayon, and self-lining (cottons and some linens are smooth and comfortable next to the skin), consider pima cotton batiste. Although sometimes difficult to find in more than a limited color palette, pima cotton batiste is a wonderful choice. It's lightweight, absorbs perspiration, irons easily, and is cooperative to handle. It is just sturdy enough to hold its shape without becoming bulky or stiff. Whichever you choose, be sure to pre-shrink it so its treatment will be compatible with that of the fashion fabric. (I always pre-treat China silk and crepe de Chine by immersing them in lukewarm water. They sometimes waterspot, and this pre-treatment will eliminate the problem, leaving their color and texture unaffected.)

When cutting out the lining, work with smaller pieces of fabric if you can. Most linings are slippery, and establishing and maintaining grain will be far easier with a piece of fabric that isn't sliding off your cutting surface. If you've made adjustments in

the skirt and lining to encourage them to hang as they should without being joined.

Unless they are sewn to the hem of the garment, the hems of skirt and trouser linings need to be finished off in some way—the choices are serging, zigzagging, turning under and machine- or hand-stitching, or applying hem lace.

You will be able to reduce bulk at the waistline if you attach the lining to the bottom of a contour waistband instead of at the waistline. In addition, the little bit of extra weight that the lining provides will encourage the facing to stay in place (see the photo at right).

Jacket linings

Tight-fitting jacket sleeves are much more comfortable to wear if they're lined. They will also slide on and off more easily. (If you don't use a lining, be sure to calculate wearing ease.)

If the jacket will have shoulder pads, be sure you have adjusted the lining for them. If they're sandwiched between the lining and the fashion fabric, the lining needs to be smaller along the shoulder seams and the top of the sleeve cap.

If the lining of a jacket seems to be bunching under the arm, try raising the seamlines of the lining's underarm seam (on both the sleeve and the body of the jacket) by ⅝ in. Double-check that the length of the sleeve is still correct. When you're inserting the sleeves into the jacket lining, put gathering stitches in the sleeve head, dart out the excess fullness, or reduce the height of the sleeve-cap area. Don't be afraid to adjust the top of the sleeve of the lining. It will pay off in a cleaner line and reduced bulk.

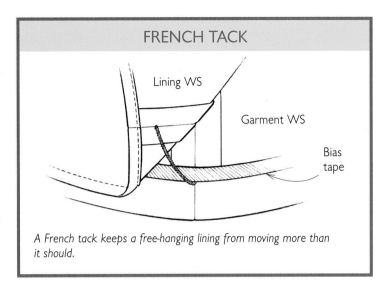

FRENCH TACK

Lining WS

Garment WS

Bias tape

A French tack keeps a free-hanging lining from moving more than it should.

Attaching a skirt lining to the bottom of a contour waistband reduces bulk at the waistline and helps the waistline stay in place.

Lining a self-faced garment

If the garment has been faced by turning back the fashion fabric's seam allowance, the lining will have to be brought up to the seamline to cover those raw edges. Staystitch the seamline of the lining, neatly trimming the seam allowance and clipping as necessary. Press the seam allowances inward and sew the lining in place with a fell stitch (it can't be machine-stitched as the fashion fabric's seam allowance has already been secured to the underlining).

SHOULDER PADS AND SLEEVE HEADS

Although many linen and cotton garments are lightweight and unstructured (or minimally structured), there are cases when additional support in the shoulder area is desirable. The underlining and the interfacing often provide sufficient internal structure, but the silhouette of the garment may call for something more.

When garments hang from the shoulders, the fit and the strength of the garment in the shoulder area are critical points to consider. Be sure to buy your pattern according to the shoulder size, because it is difficult to alter the shoulder area, while changes to the bust, waist, and hips are far simpler. Your tools for support in the sleeve and shoulder area, apart from the armscye seam allowance itself, are shoulder pads and sleeve heads. Your garment may need neither, it may need one, or it may benefit from both. As always, studying the garment carefully and trying a variety of combinations will lead you to a workable solution. Although most of us are comfortable with our understanding of shoulder pads, the use of sleeve heads is less familiar.

Sleeve heads

Although they are often overlooked, sleeve heads can be just as important to the structure and silhouette of a garment as shoulder pads. Sleeve heads fill out, and sometimes strengthen, the area at the top of the sleeve cap. A beautiful shoulder that caves in at the top of the sleeve can easily be filled out with a sleeve head. A hollow often forms where the shoulder stops and the sleeve begins, and while the seam allowance sometimes provides sufficient filling, there are times when something more substantial is called for.

Sleeve heads vary from narrow padded bias strips that are placed along the upper armscye, to an extra layer of stiffening fabric that echoes the sleeve cap, to distinct (and sometimes elaborately shaped) structures that support the entire sleeve-cap area. Examine the top of the sleeve carefully. Does the garment have a close-fitting sleeve, that has only the slightest hollow at the top of the sleeve? Then a modest sleeve head—a soft and narrow bias strip—is all that's needed. Does the garment have a gathered sleeve that needs a little more support than the fabric itself can provide? Then internal support may be called for—a layer of silk organza or net can be basted to the sleeve-cap area before the sleeve is gathered. The two layers will work as one, and the area that needs strengthening will be provided with it. Does the garment have a highly structured, pleated sleeve that needs to stand away from the body? Then a structured sleeve head is needed to fill the gap between the wearer's arm and the outer silhouette of the garment. The sleeve head must be sturdy enough to underpin the silhouette of the sleeve and support its weight.

Unlike some shoulder pads, sleeve heads generally aren't removable, so they must be able to be cared for the same way the garment is. The fabric used for narrow sleeve heads can vary from organza to hair canvas to lamb's wool. Experiment to achieve the look you want. Sleeve heads can be purchased, or you can make your own. Cut bias strips approximately 8 in. long by 2 in. to 3 in. wide and fold them in half so that one long edge is slightly wider than the other (see the top drawing on the facing page). Round the ends and hand- or machine-baste the layers together. The sleeve head is placed between the seam allowance and the top of the sleeve (see the photo on the facing page). The folded edge is placed along the armscye, with the wide side of the sleeve head against the sleeve. Place it from notch to notch, with about 5 in. of it toward the back of the sleeve and 3 in. of it toward the front. Stitch it gently in place.

If sleeve heads are needed to strengthen the entire sleeve-cap area, the choices are different. Usually lightweight, stiff fabrics do the job best. Silk organza and net are good choices (see the bottom drawing at right). You can use multiple layers if necessary. Be sure the sleeve head is soft on the underside next to the wearer's arm. The pleasure in wearing a garment will be undermined by an uncomfortable, even if effective, sleeve head.

USING STAYSTITCHING AND INNER STAY TAPE

Inner support can come from more subtle sources than interfacing and underlining. It can come from staystitching, in which a row of stitching echoes and stabilizes a seamline, or from stay tape, in which a reinforcing strip of non-stretch tape or a narrow strip of on-grain fabric does the stabilizing.

Although a row of stitching still has some give, it will lend stability until further reinforcement is added, usually in the form of a facing. And while stay tape is stronger than staystitching, the presence of a strip of tape isn't always desirable. What they both add, though, is control—they help you to tell the fabric what to do, rather than the other way around.

Staystitching

Staystitching is applied to a single layer of fabric, usually on curved (and therefore off-grain and unstable) edges. I prefer to staystitch right on the stitching line, but I do have to be very careful that any subsequent stitching doesn't stray from the stitching line and reveal the staystitching. Some sewers prefer to staystitch ⅛ in. or so to the outside of the seamline, in the seam allowance and toward the raw edge, to lessen the risk of seeing the staystitches once the seam has been sewn. Support the garment section to be staystitched as you carry it from the cutting table to the sewing machine—you

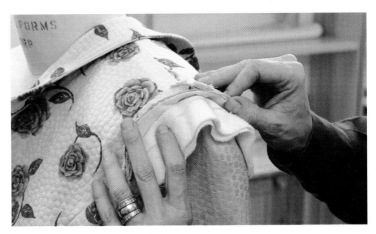

BIAS-TAPE SLEEVE HEAD

8 in. 1 in. 2 in.

You can easily make your own sleeve head with a bias strip—experiment to find the right choice of fabric or fabrics.

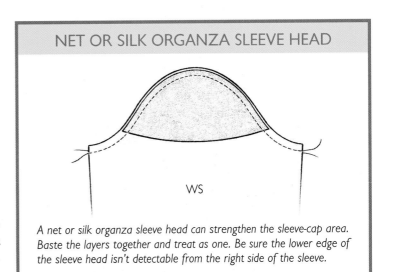

The soft bias layers of the muslin and lamb's wool sleeve head are basted into position.

NET OR SILK ORGANZA SLEEVE HEAD

WS

A net or silk organza sleeve head can strengthen the sleeve-cap area. Baste the layers together and treat as one. Be sure the lower edge of the sleeve head isn't detectable from the right side of the sleeve.

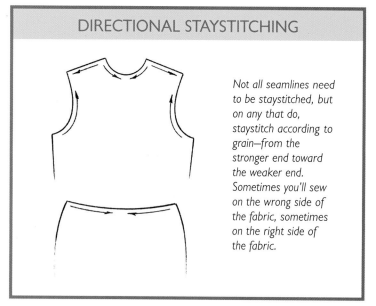

Not all seamlines need to be staystitched, but on any that do, staystitch according to grain—from the stronger end toward the weaker end. Sometimes you'll sew on the wrong side of the fabric, sometimes on the right side of the fabric.

REINFORCEMENT STITCHING WITH ORGANZA

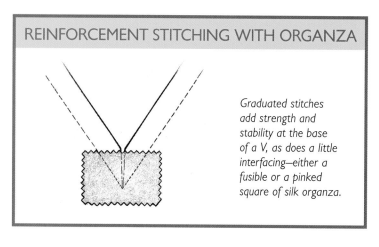

Graduated stitches add strength and stability at the base of a V, as does a little interfacing—either a fusible or a pinked square of silk organza.

of the staystitching is easy to make at this point, whereas having to remove and re-apply a facing, piping, or binding is tiresome (and sometimes impossible) and likely to distort the fashion fabric.

Staystitching can also serve as an ease stitch, allowing you to stretch or pull in a seamline as needed. It's especially useful at the waistline to ease in extra fullness. Staystitching stabilizes and defines edges that will be bound or piped; applying binding and piping will be easier and more accurate. Having a row of staystitching in place will give you the freedom to clip into a curved seamline before it's been sewn to another garment section (this is occasionally done before the seam is stitched, to better manipulate a curved seamline), without fear of distortion. Directional stay-stitching is worth considering if the fabric is particularly unstable, especially at important focal points (the neckline curve, for example). Sew first from one shoulder to the center front, then flip the fabric and sew from the other shoulder to the center front (see the top drawing at left). The same can be done at the waist seam. Although these are small details, there are situations that warrant such precise steps.

Although infrequent, there are times when you'll want to remove the staystitching once the seam has been sewn, after it's done its job. I recently staystitched the curve on a princess seam (slightly outside the seamline), and then sewed the seam. Although the seam was well sewn, the pulling-up effect of the staystitching kept the fabric from moving naturally. It wasn't until I removed the staystitching that the princess seam loosened up and the fabric was able to resume its natural movement.

Reinforcement stitching
Reinforcement stitching, a sort of concentrated staystitching, is used when unusual strain or demands are placed on a specific area of a garment—at the corner of a

don't want its own weight to pull it out of shape before you've had a chance to stabilize it. Be sure to feed the fabric into the machine gently, without distorting it.

Staystitching is especially critical with loosely woven fabrics, and you should shorten your stitch length to add even more stability. Staystitching curved seamlines not only defines and stabilizes them, but it will also give you the chance to double-check that they've been placed exactly where you want them. A small correction in the curve

square seam, at the base of a V, at the top of a godet, or at the corners of a gusset. All can benefit from the stability that small, reinforcing stitches can give. Shorten the stitches on either side of the critical area and sew directly on the seamline.

Sometimes the technique is carried a step further and a small piece of interfacing fabric is put under the area. Bias-cut silk organza is a good choice, as is a spot of fusible interfacing, as long as its presence isn't detectable from the right side of the fashion fabric. If the interfacing is a different color from the fashion fabric and its matching thread, the contrast can make it easier to see—and accurately place—machine stitches.

Stay tape

Certain seams are obvious candidates for stay tape: shoulder seams, curved pocket seams, a waistline with a shaped facing instead of a waistband, a hip curve with a side zipper. After staystitching (and early on, before any stretching can take place), apply stay tape. It can be sewn in by hand or machine, or it can be fused, as long as it is lightweight and won't stretch. Twill tape, a narrow piece of selvage, or even a narrow length of ribbon are all workable choices (a strip of silk organza selvage is my favorite choice). You can apply the tape as you sew the seam, but I usually prefer the greater accuracy of pinning and basting it in place first (quickly, with a running stitch, by hand) or, if a fusible, ironing it in place. Be sure that once applied and folded (which it will be, once the seam is sewn and finished), your stay tape doesn't create an unwanted ridge.

If you are using a fusible, be sure to use something narrow—you want to control only the seamline, not the surrounding area. Use stay tape around V necklines, which are generally cut on the bias (see the bottom photo above). Fit the neckline carefully, then apply stay tape to prevent

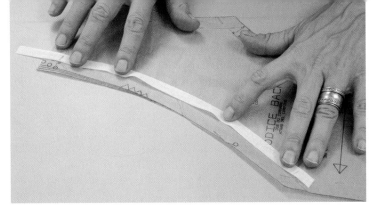

Check the length of the stay tape against the paper pattern. The fabric may already have stretched.

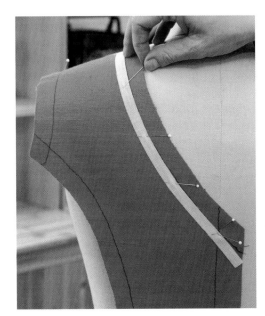

On-grain stay tape will stabilize the bias of a neck edge.

stretching. If a seamline has already stretched (along a shoulder seam, for example), refer back to your paper pattern for an accurate measurement (see the top photo). A row of staystitching will allow you to "pull in" the stretch and return the seamline to its original measurement.

Like so much in the process of sewing, there is no substitute for experimentation. You'll acquaint yourself with unfamiliar possibilities, and you'll become a careful observer as you weigh and measure the options. And the discerning eye you develop will lend itself to all aspects of your sewing.

7 | Decorative Details

One of the primary delights of working with linen and cotton is the ease with which these fabrics accommodate stylistic details. From pleats, gathers, and godets to simple and not-so-simple stitching treatments, from details that are functional to those that are simply decorative, they are all a joy to sew when worked in linen and cotton. As usual, you will need to experiment, but you will find these fabrics to be accepting and encouraging of your efforts; and I guarantee you will be delighted with the results. These techniques all work so beautifully in linen and cotton that it would almost be a shame not to incorporate some of them into your garment's design.

PLEATS

Whether you are creating delicately stitched tucks on a cotton batiste camisole or well-defined, bodied folds on a heavy linen skirt, pleats are a pleasure to incorporate into cotton, and especially linen, garments. Pleats can be the principal design element of a garment (a fully pleated skirt, for example) or merely a small, functional detail (a kick pleat, doubled perhaps, at the back of a skirt). Their charm is that they control fullness, yet not completely, revealing themselves as the wearer moves. For pleats to be a success, they must be well matched to the fabric, patiently measured and stitched, and carefully pressed and hemmed. And although I sometimes find them time-consuming to decide upon and figure out, I'm always pleased with the result.

Begin, as always, by asking yourself what it is you're after. Sharp, tight knife pleats? Deep and generous unpressed box pleats? Double pleats with a contrasting underlay? Pleats that hide pockets? Subtle pleats? Bold pleats? Assess your fabric to see what it likes to do. Some cottons resist pleating, and although the front and back fold lines can be stitched to define the folds, unpressed pleats may be a better choice. Visually, pleats emphasize the vertical. Uniformity is essential, so careful marking and stitching are crucial. Gravity plays a role, too, and if pleats are to hang as they should, the fabric has to be perfectly on grain and heavy enough to keep them in place.

I always had difficulty creating and measuring pleats until I became familiar with their terminology (see the drawing at right). Knowing the very logical names for the parts of the pleats helps me envision them, calculate and mark them, form them, and adjust them. A pleat has a front fold and a back fold; it has width, and it has depth. Whenever you're working with pleats, these are the elements you will need to think about and manipulate:

- the leading edge

- the fold line at the front of the pleat

- the fold line at the back of the pleat

- the pleat width

- the space between pleats, from leading edge to leading edge

- the placement line

- the line onto which the leading edge, or the fold line, is placed.

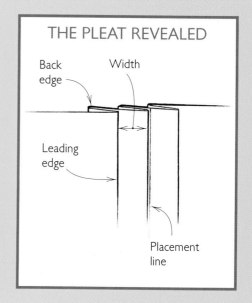

THE PLEAT REVEALED

Back edge

Width

Leading edge

Placement line

Since pleats are often added to an existing unpleated design, a lot of careful groundwork has to be done. (If pleats are new to you, refer to the sidebar above for the basics.) I work out complicated pleat formations using paper, cut either to duplicate the pleats exactly or reduced in scale. Paper folds well (better than fabric), so it's easy to mock up ideas.

Once you've worked out the proportions of your pleats and clearly established where the fold lines will be, transfer your marks to the fashion fabric. Try to work on a surface large enough to hold the entire garment. Calculate the joins in the fabric so that seamlines fall at the back edges of the pleats. Mark carefully and thoroughly, including the unstitched end of the fold lines. There are lots of folds and much to line up and match; you may find marking with more than one color will lessen the confusion. Pleats can be formed from the right side of the fabric or the wrong side; one may make more sense to you than the other. Baste thoroughly.

If the pleats are unstitched, pull up the back folds very, very slightly at the waistline and baste them carefully in place (see the top drawing on the facing page). This slight adjustment will discourage the pleats from spreading open. If pleats are stitched down, bulk at the waistline can be pared down by trimming away the excess fabric above the opening of the pleat (see the middle drawing on the facing page) or by forming the pleat from an underlay, or extension.

First fit a pleated skirt around the hips, then adjust its circumference upward toward the waist. Small adjustments to the pleats can be made unobtrusively (they can be made deeper, or the placement of their leading edges can change). When working with a plaid, determine its prominent feature and choose the width and depth of your pleats to emphasize it. A row of edgestitching along the back edge of a pleat will emphasize and strengthen the fold (see the bottom drawing on the facing page).

Pleat variations

Pleats aren't always formed in the traditional way of overlapping a fold of fabric. They can also be incorporated into an opening in the seamline (see the drawing at left on p. 96), a placement that allows several variations. The extensions can form the pleat, in combination with an underlay; or the edges of the opening can be faced, and the facings, with an underlay, can form the pleat. The seams that join the extensions, or facings, to the underlay will form well-defined back edges.

Other variations to consider include a double underlay that is hidden until the wearer moves (see the photo on p. 96), facings and/or an underlay of a different color, or a plaid underlay on the bias, stabilized with fusible interfacing.

Lining pleated garments

Pleated cotton and linen garments are seldom lined because the pleats themselves usually provide sufficient opacity. A lining can be modified from the garment, however, and cut without pleats, constructed to provide adequate movement. One option is a partial lining, which doubles as a stay (see the drawing at right on p. 96). The partial lining is joined to the skirt at the waistline and goes down to the top of the pleats. It will keep seam allowances in place and prevent the tops of the pleats from sagging. The top of the skirt and the lining/stay must be perfectly aligned, and there should be no pulling or bagging between the layers.

Hemming pleated garments

Hemming pleats can be a challenge. Except in the case of unpressed pleats, the length of the garment needs to be determined before the pleats are set. Further, seamlines often fall at the back edge of a pleat, where the seam allowance is either unpressed or pressed to one side.

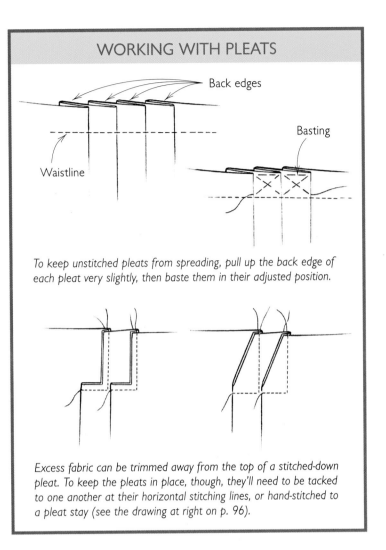

WORKING WITH PLEATS

To keep unstitched pleats from spreading, pull up the back edge of each pleat very slightly, then baste them in their adjusted position.

Excess fabric can be trimmed away from the top of a stitched-down pleat. To keep the pleats in place, though, they'll need to be tacked to one another at their horizontal stitching lines, or hand-stitched to a pleat stay (see the drawing at right on p. 96).

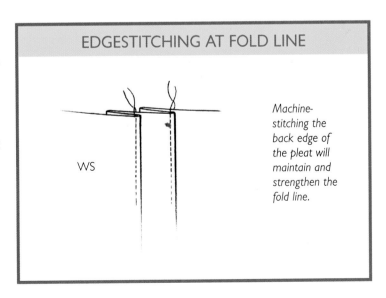

EDGESTITCHING AT FOLD LINE

WS

Machine-stitching the back edge of the pleat will maintain and strengthen the fold line.

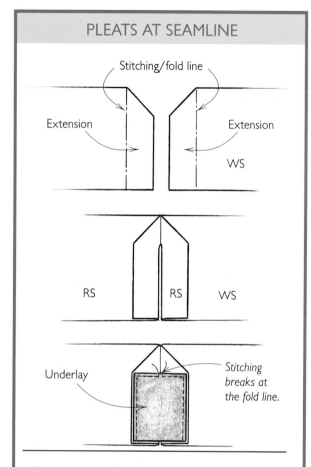

PLEATS AT SEAMLINE

Stitching/fold line

Extension

Extension

WS

RS RS WS

Underlay

Stitching breaks at the fold line.

The extensions, which could have been created from sewn-on facings, fold back along the stitching line. An underlay is sewn on three sides, and the pleat is formed.

A double-underlay pleat in a plaid linen skirt.

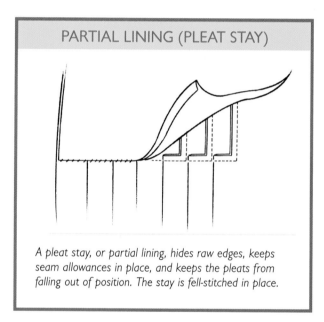

PARTIAL LINING (PLEAT STAY)

A pleat stay, or partial lining, hides raw edges, keeps seam allowances in place, and keeps the pleats from falling out of position. The stay is fell-stitched in place.

To reduce bulk, spread open the seam allowances at the back edge of a pleat at the hem (see the drawing on the facing page). Make a diagonal clip in the seam allowance at the point at which the top edge of the hem allowance falls. Press the seam allowances open below the clip, down to the bottom edge of the garment. Fold the hem allowance up carefully, keeping the seam allowances open, and sew the hem. After hemming, edgestitch the hem allowance along the back edge of the pleat to emphasize the fold and to ensure that the seam allowances stay in place.

Pressing pleated garments

Pleats can be pesky to press—but cleanly pressed pleats are the only way to show off your careful efforts. It's important to support, or at least control, the overhanging fabric when you press, or it will distort the pleats you're working on. I often pin the section I'm working with onto the ironing board, making sure that the fabric has cooled before I move onto the next section.

Although it's time-consuming, tucking brown paper strips under the pleats is worth the trouble. It will prevent ridges from forming, which really would spoil the look of the pleats. Pleats can also be set with a 50/50 mixture of white vinegar and water; once the fabric dries, the smell of the vinegar disappears.

GATHERS

Although pleats offer a controlled way to manage extra fabric, a burst of beautifully full, evenly worked cotton or linen gathers is a handsome alternative. The effect can range from the crisply buoyant and dramatic gathers of a full cotton organdy sleeve to the soft, drapey, and gentle gathers of a lawn skirt, and anything in between. I can't think of anything more fun—and rewarding—to gather than cotton and linen, and a little bit of preparation and care when creating them will ensure perfect results.

What effect are you after? Dramatic or subtle? Lush or crisp? A bold statement or a small detail? Choose the depth and fullness of your gathers accordingly. Depth is a critical decision. The deeper the gathers are, the less full they'll appear. As gathers deepen, their proportions change, and their weight pulls them down. A ratio of 2:1 is the minimum for any sort of an effect. A 3:1 ratio gives nice, full gathers; the lighter weights of cotton and linen can be gathered up to a 5:1 or 6:1 ratio. The fuller the gathers, the easier they are to work with. It's difficult to make skimpy gathers look attractive, and it's hard to stitch them evenly. As always, make up a number of samples before you decide on the final proportions for your garment.

Consider cutting gathers on the bias. If you double the fabric, the fold will be at the outer edge (eliminating the need for a further edge finish), and the raw edges will be at the seamline. Bias-cut fabric gathers willingly, with a graceful built-in curve along the outer edge.

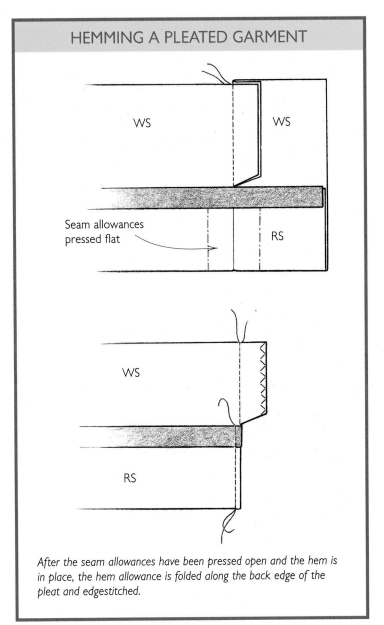

HEMMING A PLEATED GARMENT

After the seam allowances have been pressed open and the hem is in place, the hem allowance is folded along the back edge of the pleat and edgestitched.

Before gathering, mark placement lines on the fabric to be gathered and at matching points on the fabric to which it will be sewn. Notches and chalk are often difficult to find once the gathers have been formed; make thread markers in a contrasting color instead. They won't disappear, and you won't have to waste time searching for them.

GATHERS WITH THICK SEAM ALLOWANCES

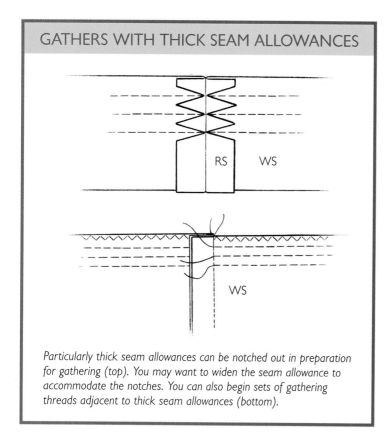

RS   WS

WS

Particularly thick seam allowances can be notched out in preparation for gathering (top). You may want to widen the seam allowance to accommodate the notches. You can also begin sets of gathering threads adjacent to thick seam allowances (bottom).

STITCHING GATHERS

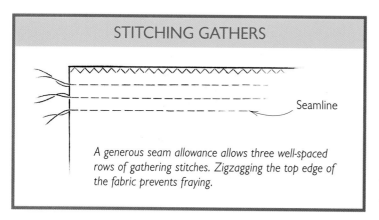

Seamline

A generous seam allowance allows three well-spaced rows of gathering stitches. Zigzagging the top edge of the fabric prevents fraying.

Before starting to gather, check that there's adequate thread in the bobbin and on the spool. Experiment with stitch length; you'll want your stitches to be long enough to be able to be pulled and manipulated, but small enough to hold the fabric in place.

Check how the threads pull over thick areas (seam allowances, for example). If thick seam allowances are a problem, try notching out part of the seam allowance, where the threads cross, or begin the gathering stitches at the seamline, without incorporating the seam allowances (see the top drawing at left). Of course, you'll have to start new threads at every seam, but it may be necessary if the larger stitches needed to accommodate thick seam allowances don't provide the control you need.

Begin by placing a row of zigzag stitches along the raw edge; you'll be doing a lot of manipulating of the seam allowance, and there's bound to be fraying if the edge isn't contained. Then sew three rows of gathering stitches—one on the seamline and the other two in the seam allowance, evenly spaced between the seamline and the raw edge (see the bottom drawing at left).

When sewing gathers, the wrong side of the fabric is usually placed face up, allowing you to follow a marked seamline and to control seam allowances. The bobbin threads tend to be a little looser than the top threads and are therefore the ones that are usually pulled.

Pull the gathering threads evenly and work them back and forth with your fingernail until the gathers are evenly lined up. The more you manipulate them, the more cooperative they'll become. Pulling the fabric will help line them up. Grasp the edge of the seam allowance with one hand and the body of the fabric with the other and pull the gathers straight.

Once you're happy with the look and spacing of the gathers, anchor the long, pulled threads around a pin. Then press the seam allowance flat, taking care not to press below the seamline (see the photo at left on the facing page). Pressing will reduce bulk at the seam allowance and encourage the gathers to stay in position until they are stitched.

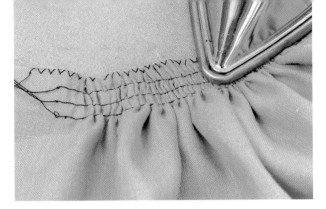

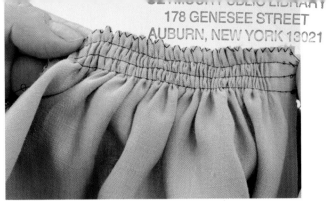

Pressing the seam allowance of the gathers helps flatten it and keep the gathers in position until they are stitched.

The bottommost pulled thread will serve as your placement and stitching guidelines.

When it's time for the gathers to be stitched into place, the lowest of the three pulled threads will form a clear, taut stitching guideline. Sometimes I prefer to pull the threads from the other side, giving me tight, sharp gathers right along the seamline on the right side of the fabric. It's a little trickier to sew them accurately, though, as the taut thread isn't visible as a guideline when you stitch the gathers in place (see the right photo above).

Gathers can be pinned or basted in place. If you pin, use plenty of pins, removing them just as the sewing-machine needle reaches them. There's no need to remove the gathering threads once the gathers have been stitched into place, but you will want to shorten the pulled threads and knot them. The seam allowance doesn't need any further treatment, as its raw edge has already been finished off with a zigzag stitch. (Trimming would result in a thick, unwelcome edge.) Examine the results of your stitching carefully—a few poorly stitched gathers can ruin the entire row. Don't be afraid to restitch a small section or two until the result is perfect.

Occasionally, gathers (especially sleeve gathers) need more support than the fabric itself can give, in which case a firm layer of fabric can be added in the sleeve-cap area. Silk organza and net are good choices; make sure, though, that the stiffening fabric

doesn't scratch the wearer. You may need a buffer—the lining will do—between the stiffening fabric and the wearer's arm.

If more than one layer of fabric has been gathered, extra fullness can be created by pulling the layers apart. The closer up to the gathering line you separate them and the sharper you pull, the fuller the gathers will be.

GODETS AND ANGLED SEAMS

While most seamlines are either straight or curved, occasionally they're angled—that is, at some point the seamline incorporates an angle. The angle can be acute—as in the point at the top of a godet—or it can be broad—as in a shallow V waist. But regardless of the degree of the angle, the technique of incorporating it into the seamline is the same. A little careful preparation and stitching will guarantee perfectly matched edges and a clear, crisp point.

Cotton and linen present the perfect canvas for these specially shaped seams: They're cooperative to manipulate and easy to stitch, with little bulk, stretching, or shifting. In fact, if you wanted to master seam-related details such as these, you'd probably stitch samples in cotton and linen first. Both elements—the godet itself and the fabric into which it will be

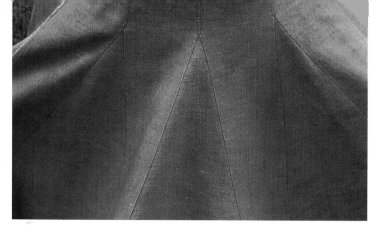

A red linen skirt with godets.

inserted—require some preparation before they're joined.

Godets are triangular inserts, usually set into the hem of a skirt, that lend weight and swing without adding bulk at the waistline or hip area. The fabric of the garment is split, and a triangular wedge is inserted. Godets create an undulating fullness, different from the orderly nature of pleats (see the photo at left).

First, the godet needs to be stabilized by staystitching (see the top drawing at left). Godets are usually cut on the straight of grain, but as they're triangular in shape, their side edges are off grain. Staystitching will not only stabilize the edges of the godet but also mark the stitching lines and the match point (the point at the top of the godet that needs to match the top of the split in the garment).

The base fabric must be prepared as well, before it's cut open. Staystitching along what will become the seamlines is the first step. A long, narrow V is sewn—not so narrow that the seam allowances become too small to work with, but not so wide that the seams become too off grain. Shorten your stitches on either side of the match point, and if the V is particularly narrow, stitch two horizontal stitches at the very top of the V before starting down the other side. If the fabric is at all loosely woven, interface the V with a small square of silk organza (or fusible, as long as it's undetectable from the right side) at the top, sewing through both layers as you staystitch (see the bottom drawing at left).

Once the V has been stitched, it can be split—cut right up into the point as far as you can with your smallest, sharpest scissors (you want your cutting line to be sharp, without any fraying). You're now ready to insert the godet. The traditional method—a continuous line of stitching that pivots at the V—can distort the fabric and be difficult to stitch accurately. Instead, you will

STABILIZING THE GODET

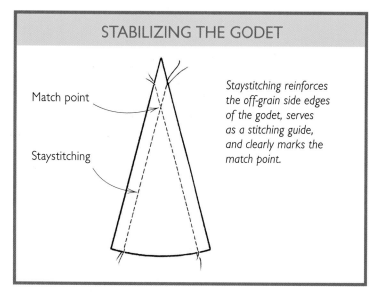

Match point

Staystitching

Staystitching reinforces the off-grain side edges of the godet, serves as a stitching guide, and clearly marks the match point.

PREPARING THE BASE FABRIC FOR A GODET

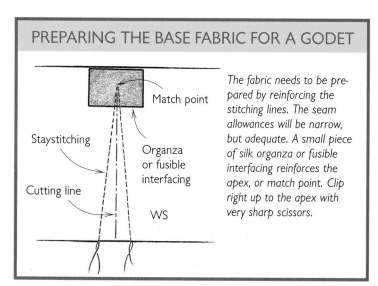

Match point

Staystitching

Organza or fusible interfacing

Cutting line

WS

The fabric needs to be prepared by reinforcing the stitching lines. The seam allowances will be narrow, but adequate. A small piece of silk organza or fusible interfacing reinforces the apex, or match point. Clip right up to the apex with very sharp scissors.

sew the godet in two passes—one for each side. Rather than pivoting, your two rows of stitches will cross at the match point and extend into the seam allowance of the godet.

With the godet on the bottom (right side up), pin the matching edge of the garment to its left side. Pin the layers together carefully at the match point, and then back along the rest of the seamline. Stitch toward the match point, starting at the base of the garment and the godet (see the top photo at right). Once the match point has been reached and stitched, swing the garment fabric out of the way and continue stitching the final small amount of the seam allowance of the godet only, using the staystitching line as your guide. Half of the godet is now sewn.

For the second half, with the godet still on the bottom, swing the garment fabric to the left and pin the other half of the garment seamline to the right side of the godet. Pin the match point carefully, and then pin the remaining seamline. Starting at the edge of the seam allowance and following the staystitching line, begin stitching on the godet only. When you reach the match point, you'll start sewing both layers—the garment and the godet. Continue until you've reached the bottom of the seamline. The godet is now inserted—cleanly and accurately.

If the fabric is at all heavy or loosely woven, partially insert the godet; that is, sew it only a few inches on either side of the V. Then let the garment and the godet hang, allowing the off-grain edges of the godet to stretch out before sewing the rest of the seamlines. Godets can also be inserted into an existing seamline—in which case the stitching goes to, but not through, the seam allowances at the match point. Backstitch the base of the opening before inserting the godet, and mark the godet as usual with staystitching.

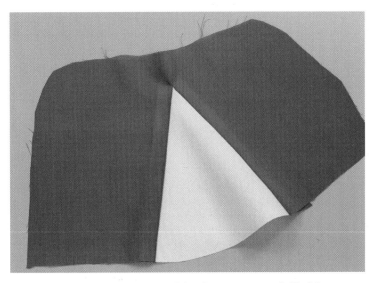

With the godet on the bottom and the skirt on top, one half of the godet is inserted (top). Sewing in the opposite direction but still with the godet on the bottom, the second half of the godet is inserted (center). The right side of the completed godet (bottom).

Multiple layers of stitching are used along the neck band of this cotton piqué dress.

You many never need a godet in your garments, but if you sew regularly you are bound to encounter angled seams, and the same techniques apply. First prepare the sections with staystitching and clipping. Then, with the pointed section on the bottom (a godet, a bodice with a V at the waist, etc.), sew the seam in two sections— first one side, then the other. You'll never again fear an angled seam, nor dread a puckered, poorly aligned V.

TOPSTITCHING

Topstitching is a pleasure to apply to cotton and linen. Carefully prepared and stitched, the results will be clear and even, with none of the slipping, shifting, and unevenness that often mars topstitching applied to less stable fabrics. Topstitching is a wonderful combination of form and function—it highlights structural lines and design details, and it keeps seam edges crisp and underlying layers in place (see the photo above).

There are decisions to be made, though. You must select from the endless varieties of thread type and color, stitch size and spacing, internal padding, and tension. There are also variations in needles and presser feet to consider. Whenever you add stitching to fabric—and especially multiple layers of stitching—its effect goes beyond the visual. The hand, or feel, of the fabric

changes. That's why you must assess the effect of the stitching carefully, so that the result you get is the result you want.

Needles

Be sure to use a new needle when topstitching. Although you can topstitch with an ordinary needle, special topstitching needles are often used. Topstitching needles are extra sharp, with a long eye to accommodate heavy thread. The long eye minimizes friction and reduces fraying, a special concern with metallic threads.

Thread

Regular thread can be, and often is, used for topstitching, However, thicker thread will make the topstitching more noticeable. You can use double thread—experiment to see if your machine prefers the two threads to work together or independently at the tension discs.

Silk buttonhole twist is a wonderful choice for topstitching on cotton and linen—it's the perfect thickness, and its subtle sheen will call just the right level of attention to the stitching (see the top photo on the facing page). Be sure to buy an adequate amount of it, though—it often comes on small 10-yd. spools. Experimentation may use more thread than you think, so purchase extra. It may be difficult or impossible to match if you run short.

With topstitching, it's not necessary to use a decorative thread in the bobbin as well. Check, though, to be sure the threads you use are compatible. You'll probably have to adjust the tension. Be sure there is plenty of thread on the spool and in the bobbin—you don't want to have to interrupt the rhythm of your careful stitching by having to rethread in the middle of a row. If you do run out of thread, insert the needle exactly where you left off and carefully bury the thread tails later. Check that the thread you choose is compatible with the garment's laundering and pressing requirements.

Marking

You'll need to create some sort of a stitching guide—it can be as simple as finding something on the presser foot to guide you. You can make tiny adjustments in the placement of the topstitching to match an easy-to-follow guideline on the foot.

You can also mark with chalk, a sliver of soap (the soap will disappear once it's ironed), or topstitching tape. If you mark with basting thread and stitch right over it, the basting threads can be stubborn and tedious to pull out, and the pulling can distort the stitched area.

Stitch length

One of the most important of the variables associated with topstitching is the stitch length. While shorter stitches will appear to be straighter, the finished row of stitching will resemble a straight line rather than separate stitches. A larger-than-usual stitch size will make the stitches more distinct, especially if the tension is adjusted so that the stitches sink down into the fabric.

For another effect, use a contrasting color of bobbin thread and adjust the tension so that just the slightest bit of it is visible between the stitches. The topstitching will look like a row of clearly defined, separate stitches (see the middle photo at right).

Padding

Although topstitching (and especially multiple rows) will add body, the effect of depth can be enhanced with interfacing (see the bottom photo at right), flannel, or even fleece. Further, fusible interfacing added to the area to be topstitched will

Silk buttonhole twist is used for the topstitching on this waistband detail.

Adjusted so that the bottom thread is visible between each stitch, the topstitching looks like a line of separate stitches.

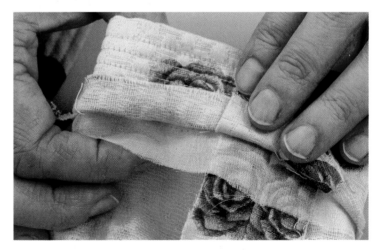

A layer of silk organza adds stability and a little bit of loft to the topstitching.

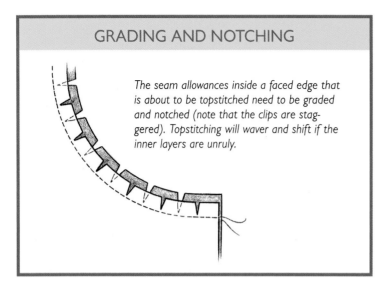

The seam allowances inside a faced edge that is about to be topstitched need to be graded and notched (note that the clips are staggered). Topstitching will waver and shift if the inner layers are unruly.

Along the edge of a jacket, the favoring changes at the base of this collar. The topstitching reinforces the change.

stabilize it and keep the weight of the presser foot from distorting the layers and shifting them.

Stitching

Almost all of the machine stitching we do on a garment is hidden—and while accuracy is important, it doesn't require the

perfect placement that topstitching does. Before you begin, make sure that your machine lighting doesn't cause shadows that make it difficult to see the stitching or the stitching guidelines. You may want to supplement your machine's ordinary lighting—good lighting, without shadows, is essential for accuracy. There can be a considerable amount of topstitching on a garment, and your eyes will tire quickly if they're constantly having to search for the stitches.

If the presser foot is applying too much tension, try to adjust it, or use a walking foot. Lifting the presser foot every few inches will allow the fabric to settle naturally, without being pushed out of shape. Before stitching, grade and notch seam allowances on any curved areas to lessen bulk (see the drawing at left). Press thoroughly before topstitching, and be scrupulously careful that any seamlines that have been favored do so consistently.

Topstitching is sometimes applied early in the construction process, without the extra layers of fabric from facings and seam allowances. Placement is easier to control with less bulk and without varying amounts of thickness. If you've applied extensive topstitching to a garment section before construction, check it against the pattern piece and expect to remark it. The stitching will probably have pulled it up, and it will be smaller.

Stitch carefully—set your machine motor at half speed if you can. Topstitching is something you want to get right the first time—you don't want to have to take it out and redo it. Stitch slowly—your machine will behave better and your stitches are more likely to be consistent if you do. Be especially careful to keep the topstitching straight when the number of fabric layers changes. If you're sewing over a particularly thick area, use a shim (a folded piece of cardboard will do) under the heel of the foot as you approach a thick area, and then under the toes of the foot as you stitch through and move away from a thick area.

To minimize dragging and shifting, hold the fabric taut as you stitch (though not so firmly that you distort the size of the stitches). Don't backstitch as you sew; instead, leave 6-in. thread tails at each end of each row, and tie them off and bury them before starting the next row. This can be a tedious part of the process, especially if there are multiple rows of topstitching—five rows of topstitching will leave 20 thread tails to be buried (two on each end of each row). Tie off as you go; otherwise, the long, loose threads (see the top photo at right) are likely to get caught in the machine.

Always stitch parallel rows in the same direction, and press after every row, holding the iron at a right angle to the stitching line (see the bottom photo at right). Be careful not to distort the fabric as you press—simply press the stitches down into the fabric. If you are channel stitching (applying a number of parallel rows of stitching), experiment ahead of time to assess the effect on the garment's drape and hand. You may want to adjust inner layers—with a lighter facing and/or interfacing.

Patch pockets are usually topstitched before they're attached to the garment. Although the topstitching may appear to be holding the pocket in place, it's usually hidden stitches that do the work.

Hems can be topstitched, although the hand of the fabric will change subtly or markedly, depending on the number of rows of stitching that have been applied.

Finishing

Finish up your beautifully applied topstitching by removing all markings, burying any remaining thread tails, and giving it a final pressing.

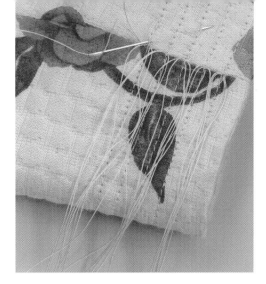

Thread tails should be dealt with after each row of stitching so they don't get caught in the sewing machine. You can see how many thread tails are created by multiple rows of topstitching. It's easiest to bury them as you go along.

Pressing topstitching at right angles to the thread eliminates distortion.

DECORATIVE STITCHING

The light weight of many cottons and linens makes them the perfect partners for delicate machine stitching and lace insertion treatments. Truly, they're made for each other. Pintucking, hemstitching, fagoting, entredeux, and lace insertion are just a few of the decorative treatments that can be applied to cotton and linen. Although they require experimentation and precise stitching, they need little in the way of specialized equipment.

If you're not familiar with these techniques, it's worth giving them a try. I guarantee you'll enjoy them—you'll find they have an understated charm all their own. Be sure to match the delicacy of the stitching and the lace with compatible seam treatments and closures. Narrow French seams are often used in this sort of work, along with small mother-of-pearl buttons.

As it's the stitching itself that is the focus of these decorative treatments, your machine must be in good condition. Clean it thoroughly before beginning; easily correctable problems can undermine the precision that's called for with decorative stitching.

If the techniques described below are unfamiliar to you, allow more than the usual amount of time for experimentation. Preparation, too, is critical. The fabric's grain must be perfectly straight. Check it before washing and pressing the fabric. If you can't see the fabric's grain well enough to cut it straight across, then pull a thread to check the grain. Try to avoid tearing the fabric—if it's at all reluctant to tear, the area around the tear will become distorted and be impossible to realign.

Wash the fabric to preshrink it and to remove any excess dyes and resins. Then starch and press the fabric, as well as all trims and laces, before stitching; they'll be much easier to control. Let the starch soak into the fabric for 20 to 30 seconds to penetrate the fibers fully before you press. If you don't, the starch will be less effective and the fabric will be likely to scorch.

If you're using polyester thread, wind it slowly. The speed under which it is wound onto the bobbin creates heat, which stretches the thread. The thread relaxes when it's sewn, and it sometimes puckers. I often hand-wind a bobbin (it takes only a few minutes) if I know the thread will be used for prominent stitching that mustn't have the slightest hint of puckering.

Hold the fabric taut while stitching, especially when sewing along its lengthwise grain. Lengthwise threads are held under much greater tension than crosswise threads and will be more likely to pucker when stitched. You may have to adjust the tension if puckering continues to be a problem.

A presser foot with a flat base will better hold the fabric in place for decorative stitching, but it will flatten out raised details. For details that incorporate raised stitching, use a grooved presser foot. The grooves will allow the stitching to pass under the foot without being flattened.

It's best to do decorative stitching on a piece of fabric larger than called for. The stitching may pull the fabric up somewhat, so leave final cutting and marking until after the decorative stitching has been applied.

As with all decorative stitching, stitch slowly and carefully, especially when using special needles. Precision is central—and essential—to the beauty of these treatments. As you gain experience, you'll become skilled at manipulating the fabric in order to stitch with precision. Tiny shifts in the position of the fabric and the placement of the stitches will result in stitching that is clear and clean, rather than muddy and hard to discern.

Twin needle pintucks

Rather than sewing narrow pintucks in the traditional manner, you can stitch them easily and accurately with a twin needle. The two rows of thread on the top of the fabric share a bobbin thread, which pulls the two rows together, forming a small ridge, or pleat. Pintucks work best on lightweight fabrics; medium and heavy fabrics pleat best in the traditional way.

Special pintucking feet are available that allow already sewn pintucks to pass undisturbed through the grooves on the bottom of the foot. The more grooves the foot has, the more possibilities you'll have for spacing. Place a just-sewn pintuck into one of the grooves; its placement will determine the width between tucks as well as serve as a guide for stitching subsequent tucks.

Thread the machine carefully. The threads may or may not separate at the tension disks, but they must clearly separate as they are threaded into the twin needles. The pintucks can be given further definition if they're corded—that is, if a narrow cord is incorporated into the tuck. The cord is threaded into the small hole on the needle plate and becomes automatically inserted into the ridge as the tuck is sewn. Colored cord (be sure it's colorfast) will lend a subtle touch of color and more definition (see the top photo at right).

Pintucks are often left unpressed. To press the fabric between them, place them along the edge of the ironing board so that the fabric between the rows can be reached with the tip of the iron.

Hemstitching

Hemstitching, when worked by hand, is formed by pulling horizontal threads and then bundling groups of the vertical threads that remain. A similar effect can be achieved with a wing needle—an unusual-looking needle that bulges out above the point. The sharp point of the needle pierces the fabric, while the wide part creates a hole.

Zigzagging two parallel and overlapping rows of stitches with a wing needle creates the effect of hemstitching. Sew one row of zigzagging, then pivot the fabric so that the second row of zigzagging will be parallel to the first (and worked in the opposite direction). The needle will re-enter the holes of one side of the first row of zigzag stitches (see the drawing and bottom photo at right). A noticeable hole is created when the fabric has been pierced twice.

With hemstitching, placing the second row of stitches accurately is critical. Stitch as

Sewn with a twin needle, pintucks can be given further definition by inserting a cord into each row of stitching.

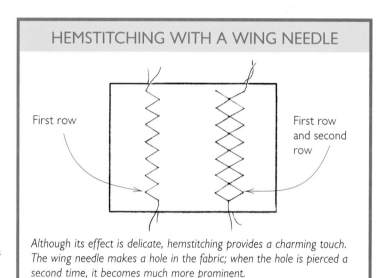

HEMSTITCHING WITH A WING NEEDLE

First row

First row and second row

Although its effect is delicate, hemstitching provides a charming touch. The wing needle makes a hole in the fabric; when the hole is pierced a second time, it becomes much more prominent.

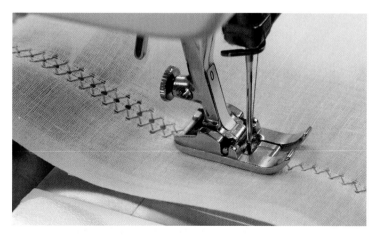

Hemstitching by machine: As the second row is zigzagged, the wing needle doubles back through one side of the stitches in the first row.

A simple zigzag stitch can be used for fagoting.

slowly as necessary (sometimes it's almost stitch by stitch) to allow the needle to re-enter the hole that was made on the first row of stitching. Use a presser foot that allows you to see the needle entering the fabric; otherwise, it will be impossible to place the stitches precisely. Although tedious to stitch, hemstitching is usually used only in limited areas; it's not too difficult to maintain accuracy and precision on a relatively short row of stitching.

Fagoting

Fagoting is a decorative stitch that holds two pieces of fabric or lace together. A space is left between the two edges as they're stitched, and the stitches go from side to side, bridging the gap (see the photo at left). Your machine may or may not have built-in decorative stitches that lend themselves to fagoting. Experiment to find a stitch that works—you may want to use something more elaborate than a zigzag.

It's somewhat disconcerting to sew in the air, with only a little bit of the stitch catching on the edges of the fabrics. You'll have to find a suitable spacer (a narrow strip of cardboard, cut from a manila folder, works well, as does a narrow plastic coffee stirrer). Practice until you're comfortable with the tolerances involved.

Entredeux

Entredeux is a ladder-looking trim often used as a bridge between fabrics or between fabric and lace. It's easy to incorporate and beautifully effective as long as the stitching used to apply it is precise. Entredeux is attached to other fabrics and trims with a zigzag stitch. Careful experimentation with the length, width, and tension of the stitching is paramount—the stitches must match the spacing of the holes in the entredeux.

JOINING ENTREDEUX TO FABRIC

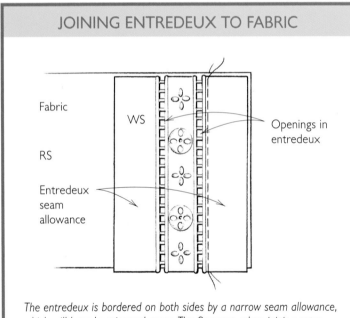

The entredeux is bordered on both sides by a narrow seam allowance, which will later be trimmed away. The first step when joining entredeux to fabric is to put right sides together and stitch just to the right of the entredeux in its seam allowance.

To join entredeux to fabric, put the right sides together and stitch just to the right of the holes of the entredeux (see the drawing on the facing page). Turn to the right side, and press the seam allowances toward the fabric (you can press the seam allowances with the iron, or you can use your fingers to manipulate them—cotton and linen are easy to finger-press). Then place a row of zigzag stitches over the seamline, adjusting their length and position to match the openings in the entredeux. Finally, trim away the seam allowance of the entredeux on the underside of the fabric.

To apply entredeux to lace, first trim the seam allowance from the entredeux (the trimmed edge won't fray). Butt the edges together and zigzag (see the drawing at right), carefully matching the length of the zigzags to the openings in the entredeux.

LACE

The intricacy and delicacy of lace make it the perfect counterpoint to cotton and linen's straightforward nature. Easy to apply by machine or hand, lace can echo a rich print with its abundance of details, or it can stand in sharp contrast to a plainer fabric.

Lightweight strips

Despite its delicate appearance, a strip of lace with two straight edges is easy to insert into cotton and linen. Carefully pin the lace into place and sew both edges with a straight stitch. Then cut the underlying fabric down the middle (be sure not to cut the lace as well), and press the seam allowances away from the lace (see the top photo on p. 110). Apply a row of zigzag stitches along each border of the lace (see the middle photo on p. 110), and finish by trimming away the remaining seam allowances. As with all decorative stitching, correct stitch width and length are crucial, as is following the border of the lace carefully and consis-

After the right side of the entredeux and fabric are stitched together, a row of precisely applied zigzag stitches finishes the process.

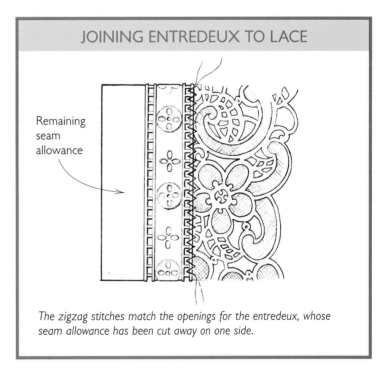

JOINING ENTREDEUX TO LACE

Remaining seam allowance

The zigzag stitches match the openings for the entredeux, whose seam allowance has been cut away on one side.

tently. This final row of stitching will create a pleasingly firm edge. The zigzag stitches you use here may be far smaller than the zigzag stitches you're used to, but delicate and unobtrusive stitching is critical.

After stitching the lace along both edges, the underlying fabric is cut down the middle and pressed back.

Apply a row of zigzag stitches along each border of the lace.

To join two pieces of lace, butt the edges and zigzag.

To join two strips of lace, simply butt their edges together and zigzag (see the bottom photo at left). Stitch slowly so that the strips neither overlap nor spread apart while being stitched.

Heavier laces

While we're accustomed to seeing narrow, straight strips of lace inset into lightweight cottons and linens (in the manner just described), lace can be combined with cotton and linen in other ways. It can be used in appliqué form (in which individual pieces of lace are attached to the fashion fabric) or in strip form (in which bands of lace decorate the fabric).

Be sure the fabric to which you're sewing the lace is colorfast and has been preshrunk (if necessary). Prepare the lace by pressing it face down into a thick terry towel. Lace seldom shrinks, but pressing will smooth it out, especially the little areas of net between the motifs of Alençon (corded) lace.

Regardless of its form, lace can be stitched on by machine (as long as it is unadorned with pearls) or by hand. Machine stitches are quicker, but hand stitches allow for greater control. If attaching the lace by machine, zigzag around the perimeter (if working with Alençon lace, straddle the cording with the stitches, as shown in the top drawing on the facing page). If attaching the lace by hand, use a fell stitch (see the bottom drawing on the facing page). Bury the backs of the stitches in an inner layer, if possible, or cover them with a lining. The result will be more attractive, and the stitches will be less likely to catch on something. After the lace has been stitched, press the area again, with the lace face down in a thick towel. It will conform beautifully to the area to which it's been sewn.

Lace appliqué

Of all the laces, Alençon and Guipure are the sturdiest for appliqués. Chantilly lace is usually too delicate to be used; in addition to its fragile nature, the discrepancy between the delicacy of the lace and the firmness of the fabric to which it will be applied can cause problems with shifting and rippling. Alençon and Guipure are wiser choices. The denser the motifs, the sturdier and more stable (and easier) the lace will be to work with. A single motif can be used, or the coverage can be lavish.

Appliqués are usually applied late in the construction process, overlaying seam allowances and abutting finished edges. Their thickness makes them undesirable in seam allowances and seamlines. And visually, it's easier to assess where to place lace once the whole of the garment can be considered.

The lace you choose will have to be separated into appliqués. Use small, sharp scissors to cut the lace apart, after examining it carefully to choose the best places to cut. The motifs of Alençon lace are fairly easy to delineate; try to cut through as few of the outlining cords as possible. The cut ends will fray eventually (overcast them to lessen the problem), so you want to keep their number to a minimum. In addition to separating the motifs from the rest of the yardage, you'll need to trim away some of the net background. Cut away as much as you can without weakening the motifs. Guipure lace motifs are usually joined with thread bars, so it's easy to separate them by cutting through the threads. Don't cut through the motifs themselves, though, as they'll fray.

Borders and bands

Fine laces almost always feature an attractive border (in the case of Alençon lace, it's scallops; in the case of Guipure lace, it's a repeating motif). It's the border that is

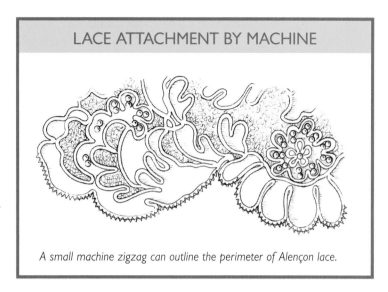

LACE ATTACHMENT BY MACHINE

A small machine zigzag can outline the perimeter of Alençon lace.

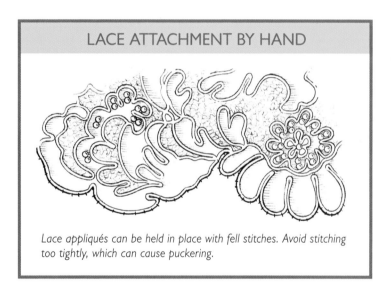

LACE ATTACHMENT BY HAND

Lace appliqués can be held in place with fell stitches. Avoid stitching too tightly, which can cause puckering.

often placed at the hemline or the bottom of a sleeve. A scalloped lace border can simply overhang a straight edge, but there will be greater stability if the underlying fabric itself is scalloped as well (see the photo at left on p. 112).

A strip or band of Alençon or Guipure lace can also be inserted into the body of the fabric. The underlying fabric can remain or be removed. If the fabric is cut away, the

An Alençon lace trim has been appliquéd over the scalloped hem.

In addition to an Alençon lace band (the edges have been machine-zigzagged and the backing fabric cut away), a narrow lace trim has been sewn at the hemline, first with a straight stitch, then with a tiny zigzag. The hem allowance will be trimmed away.

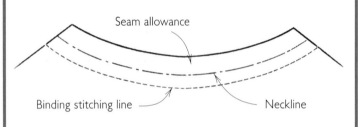

BINDING AT THE NECKLINE

Seam allowance

Binding stitching line

Neckline

If the finished edge of the binding is to rest on the neckline, it needs to be applied lower. If it were stitched onto the neckline, the finished edge would be higher (and tighter) than the neckline.

cut edges should mimic the shape of the edges of the lace, and the raw edges should be treated (see the photo at right above).

BINDING

Cotton and linen garments are ideal candidates for binding—the stable nature of these fabrics, as well as their enthusiasm for being folded, makes bound edges easy and satisfying to make. While it doesn't provide a hugely stable finish, binding does lend a beautiful definition to the edges along which it's applied. It can offer merely a sug-

gestion of an edge finish, or it can make a bold or even contrasting statement.

Bindings are often used in place of facings. They lack the strength that a facing provides and give no support for the surrounding area the way a facing does, but there are instances when nothing more than an attractive edge finish is necessary. It sounds easy—cut a bias strip, fold it, and stitch it in place. But there's really more to it than that; and as usual, careful preparation will build in the control that guarantees beautifully shaped, perfectly even bias trim.

Binding is often used at the neckline, where placement, contour, and comfort are critical. Even before staystitching, calculate to make sure that your binding will be placed exactly where you want it to be (see the drawing at left).

On a faced neckline, the finished edge is along the seamline. On a bound neckline, the binding must be stitched below the seamline if the finished circumference is to be the same that a facing would provide. A binding stitched along the seamline would have its finished edge above it, and its circumference would be smaller. The difference in placement may not matter, or it may matter greatly. Just be sure to take this into consideration ahead of time, so you're not surprised by a too-high (and too-tight) neckline.

Before cutting the bias strips you need, experiment with samples of different widths and apply them in different ways. Determine also if and where the bias will need to be pieced and how it will be finished off at the ends if there's an opening. Although binding can easily be applied by machine using a binding attachment (in which case a single row of stitching applies the bias), you may decide to finish the bias by stitching unobtrusively alongside it or by topstitching it, possibly twice. You may prefer the control of combining machine and hand stitching, in which case no stitching will be visible on the right side of the garment. The top drawing at right shows a few variations.

Before the binding is applied, the underlying fabric needs to be stabilized (and the stitching line marked) by staystitching along the stitching line. If the fabric is at all loosely woven, staystitch directionally, especially at the neck edge; begin at the shoulders and stitch toward the center (see the bottom drawing at right). You'll be stitching from different sides of the garment, but it's important that there be no distortion, especially at the center front of the neckline. You can avoid distortion by supporting the weight of the garment as you stitch.

To prepare the bias strips, cut them carefully, without the slightest variation from true bias. Anything other than exactly 45° will result in uncorrectable rippling and twisting. If you plan to use bias binding often, you may want to invest in a large triangle to help you mark the bias accurately (look for one at an art supply store). When calculating the width of the bias strip, be sure to account for turn of the cloth, remembering that the thicker the fabric, the more it will be affected. For regular binding, allow four times the eventual

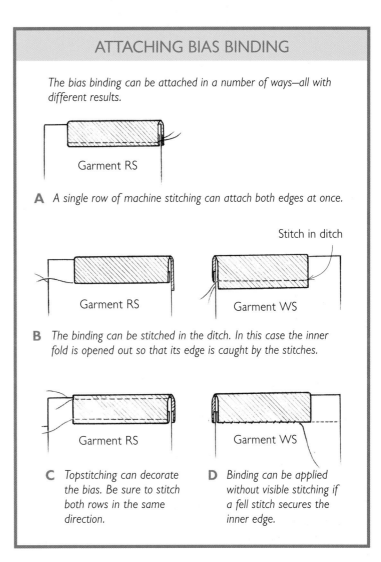

ATTACHING BIAS BINDING

The bias binding can be attached in a number of ways—all with different results.

Garment RS

A A single row of machine stitching can attach both edges at once.

Stitch in ditch

Garment RS   Garment WS

B The binding can be stitched in the ditch. In this case the inner fold is opened out so that its edge is caught by the stitches.

Garment RS   Garment WS

C Topstitching can decorate the bias. Be sure to stitch both rows in the same direction.

D Binding can be applied without visible stitching if a fell stitch secures the inner edge.

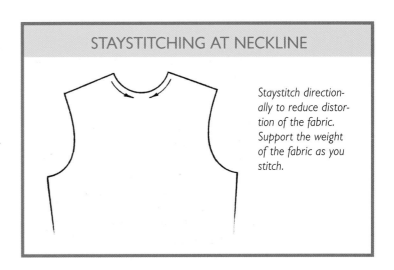

STAYSTITCHING AT NECKLINE

Staystitch directionally to reduce distortion of the fabric. Support the weight of the fabric as you stitch.

JOINING BIAS STRIPS

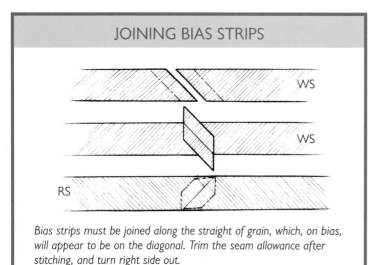

Bias strips must be joined along the straight of grain, which, on bias, will appear to be on the diagonal. Trim the seam allowance after stitching, and turn right side out.

BIAS STRIP AT AN OPENING

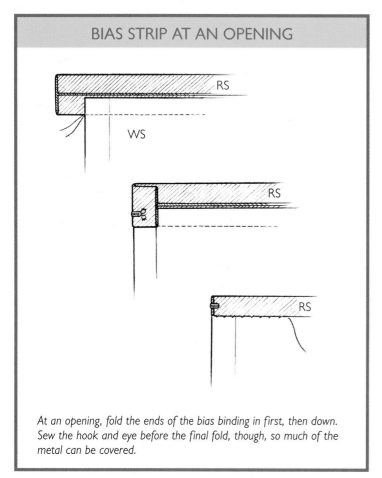

At an opening, fold the ends of the bias binding in first, then down. Sew the hook and eye before the final fold, though, so much of the metal can be covered.

desired width plus ⅛ in. to ¼ in. for turn of the cloth. Cut the strips with a rotary cutter or your sharpest, longest scissors—dull blades would distort your cutting lines. You may want to iron some of the stretch out of the bias before folding it. (Hold the iron at 90° to the strip; any other position will distort it.) Ironed, it will be easier to control, but keep in mind that the bias will be slightly narrower than before. If the bias is particularly lightweight and seems difficult to control, try starching it. Use a bias tape maker to fold the bias or do it carefully by hand.

If the bias will be pieced, you will need to determine where. It may be more attractive to make two symmetrical joins instead of one oddly placed join. Don't place joins over design details or seamlines, which are already thick. Join the bias on the straight of grain, which will appear as a diagonal line (see the top drawing at left). Carefully placed, stitched, and pressed, joins will be barely visible and not at all unattractive.

The bias can be preshaped before stitching. It can be positioned against the seamline or against the paper pattern. Shape it carefully, using light pressure and steam from the iron. Be careful not to stretch it—your goal is to shape it without distorting its width.

Whether sewing the bias entirely by machine or with a combination of machine and hand stitching, consider basting the bias into place instead of pinning it. No amount of pinning can provide the control that basting offers. The results will far outweigh the time spent.

If there's an opening, fold the ends of the bias in before folding it down into place. If you're using a hook and eye at a closure, try to cover up at least part of the metal (see the bottom drawing **at left**). The hook and eye can be sewn on before the final layer of bias is folded down into place; the fabric will cover all but the working part of the metal eye.

French bias

Most sewers are familiar with the standard bias application, but there is another way to apply a bias trim. It works especially well around necklines and with lighter weights of fabric. French bias does use more layers of fabric (seven in all) than the traditional bias application (which uses five), but the care and control with which it's applied make the difference negligible. In fact, the extra layers add just a hint of padding and softness to the bound edge.

Start with a bias strip six times the desired finished width, adding a small amount for turn of the cloth. Fold the strip in half, and lightly press it, carefully avoiding any distortion. This fold line will eventually become your hand-stitching line. Hand-baste the layers together, one-third of the way in from the raw edges (Step 1 in the drawing at right). This will become your machine-stitching line. Place the bias strip on the right side of the garment, matching the stitching lines (the staystitching on the garment and the hand basting on the bias strip). Pin it carefully, shaping it as necessary, and baste it in place (Step 2), then stitch.

Now, with the right side of the garment facing you, finger-press the bias up along the seamline. Pin it carefully, and baste again (Step 3), this time through the bias and the seam allowances. Turn the garment over, and carefully fold the bias into position (Step 4). Its folded edge will rest along the stitching line. Unless the seam allowance was trimmed down earlier, you will have to trim it now to the finished width of the bias binding. (Don't trim it too low—you don't want to form a hard, short ridge.)

Next, carefully pin the bias, placing your pins at right angles to the garment, pinning first in halves, then quarters, then eighths, and so on (Step 5). Finish by fell-stitching

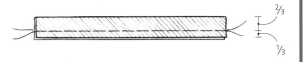

1 *Fold the bias strip in half and hand-baste one-third of the way in from the raw edges.*

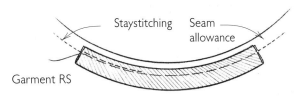

2 *Baste the strip a second time to position it along the seamline. The edges of the seam allowance and the binding don't have to align; only the staystitching lines and the basting lines must match.*

3 *Baste a third time, through the bias strip and the seam allowance, to hold the binding in place evenly and securely.*

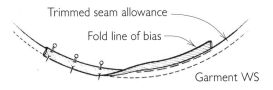

4 *On the wrong side, fold the bias strip over into place, with its folded edge resting on the stitching line.*

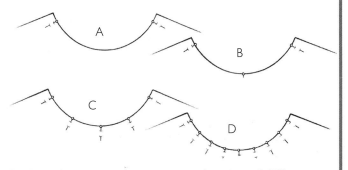

5 *Pin in the sequence shown to prevent distortion and shifting.*

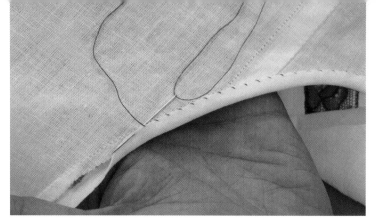

A final row of fell stitches holds the folded edge of the French binding in place.

A cotton lawn dress with a fabric-covered belt.

the bias into place (see the top photo above), positioning your stitches so they're hidden in the seam allowance of the garment. You may want to do a final gentle press of the bias, or you may decide that its natural fold provides enough definition. If you do decide to press, do so at 90° to the bias. Otherwise, all your careful work will be undermined.

ACCESSORIES

Cotton and linen are natural candidates for self-covered buttons and belts (see the bottom photo at left). Whether you're covering them yourself or having them professionally covered, take a few minutes to experiment with layering. Some cottons and linens are so lightweight that the metal or fabric base of the buttons or belt will show through, altering the color. A double layer of fabric may similarly change the color, or unwelcome designs may show through if a printed fabric has been doubled. Choose layers with care.

POCKETS

Pockets can be subtle or bold, decorative or functional. They can be a focal point or barely detectable—as simple as an unlined patch pocket or as complex as a carefully matched double welt pocket with a flap. Pockets can be loosely grouped into two categories: patch pockets (in which a piece of fabric, often square, is sewn onto the garment) and set-in pockets (in which the pocket is inserted into a seamline or an opening in the garment). Welt pockets fall into the latter category. While the patch pocket forms its own pocket bag on the surface of the garment, the set-in pocket needs a separate pocket bag on the inside of the garment.

When planning your garment, determine the pocket's role and design, and construct and place it accordingly. Consider the strain that will be placed on it, and how the underlying fabric will bear that strain. Is it a purely decorative pocket that simply rests on the fabric? Or will it bear constant use, requiring easy access and sturdy edges, firmly and securely sewn to its base? What sort of inner support will the base fabric need?

In general, tighter weaves work better for welt pockets, and looser weaves work better for patch pockets. The proper interfacing, though, can make not-so-tightly woven fabrics suitable for in-seam and even welt pockets (see the top photo at right).

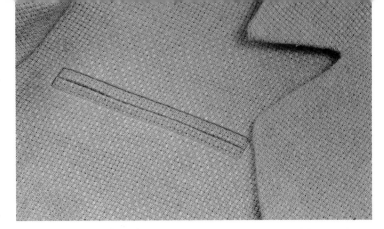

A welt pocket in a linen jacket. The fabric around the opening, as well as the welts themselves, has been interfaced.

Patch pockets

While much of your attention will be given to creating the pocket and attaching it, don't overlook preparing the area to which it will be sewn. The fabric that underlays the pocket needs to be strong enough to remain undistorted once the pocket is in place. The area under the top corners of a patch pocket is particularly vulnerable, especially if the fabric is at all loosely woven, so interface accordingly.

Check the grain carefully before cutting out the pocket. It must be perfectly straight both horizontally and vertically. If the pocket is cut on the bias, make sure that it's been stretched thoroughly before applying interfacing and staystitching.

It's critical that matching pockets be exactly the same. The easiest way to guarantee uniformity is to use a template of the pocket. Templates are essential, both to match one side of the pocket to the other and to match one pocket to another. Metal templates that feature a variety of curves are available, or you can make your own using tagboard (old manila folders are ideal). To make a template, trim the seam allowance from the tissue pocket pattern, trace the outline of the pocket onto the tagboard, and cut it out along the outline. The template will be the size of the finished pocket, so you must remember to add an adequate seam allowance when you cut out the fashion fabric, the interfacing, and the lining. Mark the fashion fabric and the interfacing (once they've been joined) and the lining with a tracing wheel and tracing paper, or with basting stitches, following the perimeter of the template (see the bottom photo at right).

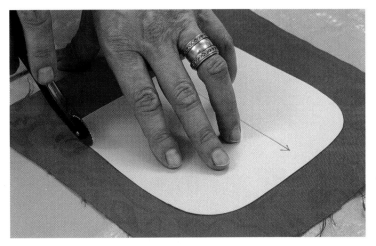

Trace around the perimeter of the pocket template with a tracing wheel.

Pockets need to be interfaced as well as lined to help them maintain their shape and to preserve the line of their upper edge. Experiment to find the best choice. The interfacing in the pocket may differ from the interfacing in other parts of the garment. You may need to add an additional layer of interfacing along the top edge.

Once the pocket has been marked, staystitch the perimeter, making sure that any curved edges match perfectly. If the lower edges are curved, they can be folded up in a number of ways. Gathering threads can parallel the curve at the corners (see the photo on p. 118). A little hand-gathering is quick to apply, and may be easier to control than machine gathering. The staystitching line can guide the fold, or the template can be

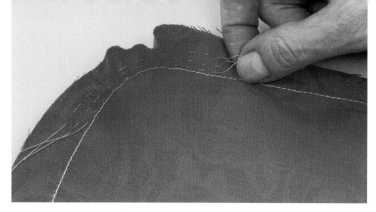

Three rows of basting stitches at the corners will be gathered to help shape the seam allowances around the edge of the pocket.

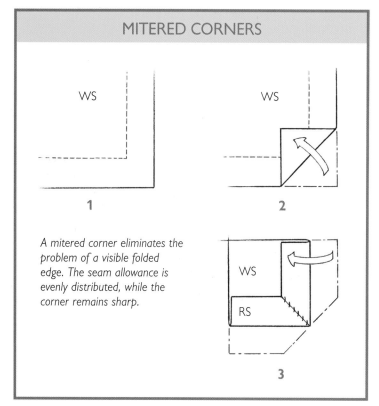

MITERED CORNERS

A mitered corner eliminates the problem of a visible folded edge. The seam allowance is evenly distributed, while the corner remains sharp.

ing it, but it would have to be trimmed quite low in order for the pinking to be effective, inviting fraying. If the lower edges are square, fold the bottom edge up first, then fold the side edges in.

Corners can also be mitered (see the drawing at left). A mitered corner sometimes controls the thickness of multiple layers better than folding one edge over the other. The mitered corner can be stitched by machine, but it's quick and accurate to stitch it by hand. Machine stitching on the miter seams, which are on the bias, can distort them. You will be better able to limit the stretch of the bias if the short mitered seam is sewn by hand.

A lining applied by hand is the best way to guarantee that the pockets will be shaped as you wish. Fell stitching can hold the lining in place. It's quick to do and holds the lining securely. You can also stitch the lining and pocket by machine. With the right sides of the lining and pocket together, stitch the edges, leaving an opening big enough to turn the right side out. Be careful that all curves match and that a crease doesn't form along the edges of the pocket between the fashion fabric and the lining. It's a difficult seam to press, and if a crease forms, the seamline won't fall exactly along the edge of the pocket. The result will be a pocket smaller than intended.

Piping can be used to outline patch pockets and add an extra decorative element. If only the sides and bottom edge of the pocket are piped, then the piping won't have to be joined to itself. If the piping surrounds the entire pocket, it will have to overlap (if so, place the overlap along an outside edge) or be pieced (a better alternative, but tricky to sew to the exact length).

Pockets are often topstitched (see the photo on the facing page), but the stitches will be more accurate if the pocket is first topstitched, then attached by hand from

used. Using plenty of steam from your iron, patiently shape the seam allowance around the template. Again, make sure that all curves match. The seam allowance can be notched, but be careful that the notches don't encourage corners to form when the seam allowance is turned up. The seam allowance could be pinked, in effect notch-

the inside of the garment. Place the pocket while trying the garment on so that it conforms to the curves and proportions of the body. Stuff a tissue in the pocket to mimic natural wearing ease.

Pin, then baste the pocket in the center (form an X with your stitches) as well as along the edges (see the top drawing at right). The pocket can be stitched on by hand, from inside the garment, with reinforcement at the upper corners (see the bottom drawing at right). It can also be attached with a blind-hem stitch (use a narrow, short stitch setting) applied to its lining. If you choose to attach the pockets this way, be sure you've stitched the lining to the pocket by machine rather than by hand.

A piped pocket edge will allow you to hide the stitches that attach the pocket to the garment. Stitch in the hollow between the piping and the fashion fabric and be sure to reinforce your stitching at the corners. If you are attaching the pocket by stitching around its edges, shorten the stitches at the curves. You will have more control over your stitches. Be sure to reinforce the upper corners.

In-seam pockets

To add an in-seam pocket along the side seam of trousers, start the opening 1 in. below the waist and finish it 7½ in. below (giving a 6½-in. opening). Add another 2½ in. to 3 in. along the bottom edge (see the top drawing on p. 120).

Vertical side front pockets, inserted into the seamline, can gap in a very unflattering way on straight skirts. In addition to being easier to insert the hand into, a diagonal pocket is more flattering than a vertical pocket. Whether the pocket opening is vertical or curved, it will need to be reinforced. This is the edge that will get stretched from use, regardless of its grain.

Topstitched patch pockets.

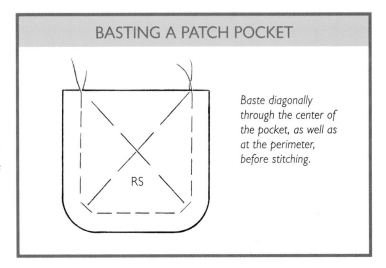

BASTING A PATCH POCKET

RS

Baste diagonally through the center of the pocket, as well as at the perimeter, before stitching.

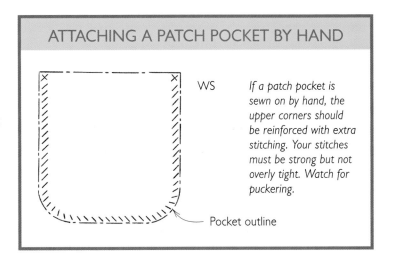

ATTACHING A PATCH POCKET BY HAND

WS

If a patch pocket is sewn on by hand, the upper corners should be reinforced with extra stitching. Your stitches must be strong but not overly tight. Watch for puckering.

Pocket outline

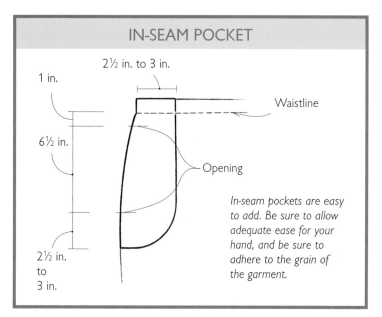

IN-SEAM POCKET

2½ in. to 3 in.

1 in.

6½ in.

Waistline

Opening

2½ in. to 3 in.

In-seam pockets are easy to add. Be sure to allow adequate ease for your hand, and be sure to adhere to the grain of the garment.

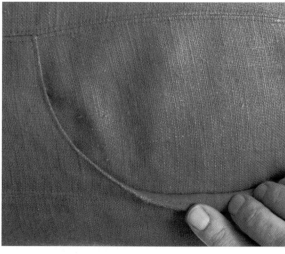

A curved, understitched pocket on a red linen skirt. The pocket has been lined with light-weight cotton.

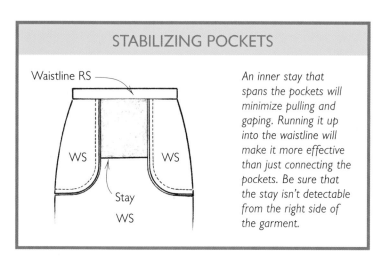

STABILIZING POCKETS

Waistline RS

WS   WS

Stay

WS

An inner stay that spans the pockets will minimize pulling and gaping. Running it up into the waistline will make it more effective than just connecting the pockets. Be sure that the stay isn't detectable from the right side of the garment.

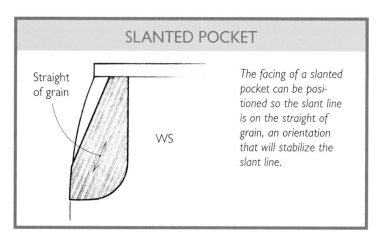

SLANTED POCKET

Straight of grain

WS

The facing of a slanted pocket can be positioned so the slant line is on the straight of grain, an orientation that will stabilize the slant line.

If the pocket opening is curved, be sure to reinforce the curve with staystitching and stay tape. Understitching the facing as well further firms and defines the edge.

Consider adding an inner stay to keep the pockets in place and to keep them from gaping. The stay will be more stable if it extends into the waistline (see the middle drawing at left). If the fashion fabric is lightweight, the pocket bags can be made from the same fabric, or a lining fabric can be used. If the fashion fabric is white, line the pockets with flesh-colored fabric to mute their presence.

Vertical in-seam pockets can be cut "in one," which means that they can extend from the garment without a seam. This approach will use more fabric, though, and the openings must still be reinforced.

If the pocket is cut on the diagonal (see the bottom drawing at left), you can stabilize the top edge of the pocket by positioning the facing's straight edge so that it's cut on

Victorian petticoats are easy to find in vintage clothing and antique shops, and many of them are still in wonderful condition. Sometimes the wearer's name is delicately written inside the waistband—my daughter owns a petticoat that once belonged to an "Anne Paine." It's a touching link to the past.

Victorian petticoats are a wonderful source of inspiration, with their wealth of carefully detailed machine work. Lace insertion is common, as are carefully stitched rows of pleats, eyelet work, and flounces of gathered lace. The cotton they're made out of is usually very sturdy, and in most cases it's thick enough to be able to wear unlined. Yesterday's ankle-length petticoats translate well into more modern, and very attractive, mid-calf-length skirts for today's taller figures. A little bit of care is all it takes to make them wearable again. These skirts can be cleaned and even gently bleached, and any imperfections that remain can be accepted as the inevitable hallmarks of their age.

Victorian petticoats are often too short and too tight at the waistband for today's wearers, but these problems are easy to remedy. For extra length, you can add a yoke that closes with a placket, a row of gathered lace at the hem, or an inset band of lace in the body of the skirt. Rows of horizontal pleats are found on many skirts; they could easily camouflage the addition of a band of fabric or lace. Victorian petticoats almost always gather at the waistline, and true to the style of the time, the gathers are often fuller at the back than at the front. The gathers can be left as they are, or respaced if the waistline needs to be altered.

Common closures for petticoats include a single button at the waist or the ties of a drawstring. A full placket of buttons wasn't necessary, as the petticoat was worn under other layers of fabric. Wearing it as a skirt, however, calls for a closure that offers more modesty—a placket that closes with delicate mother-of-pearl buttons, for example. The gentle off-white of the buttons is less glaring than metal snaps or hooks and eyes and is far more appropriate than a zipper. ■

Victorian petticoats make elegant skirts.

the straight of grain (it's usually cut on the diagonal). A further benefit of a slanted pocket is a bias pocket pouch, which will conform nicely to the body.

To guarantee that the pocket bag will fit smoothly, either try on the garment or place the garment over a curve that matches the appropriate part of the body. Smooth the layers and adjust the stitching line as necessary. The raw edges may line up exactly, but they'll probably need a little adjustment. This outer seam can be zigzagged, pinked, serged, or even bound with a strip of bias. Be sure, though, that your seam finish isn't detectable from the right side of the garment.

Press the pocket area carefully to avoid making an impression on the right side of the garment. First press the pocket bag separately, then press the top of the garment, moving the pocket bag out of the way if you can.

8 Finishing Details

Careful work throughout the planning and construction phases of a project deserves to be carried right through to the garment's completion. There are a number of finishing details, some hidden, some not, that will improve your garment in small, yet important ways.

CLOSURES

Linen and cotton present few challenges as far as ordinary closures are concerned. Centered and lapped zippers along with machine-made buttonholes are the norm, but there are a few variations worth considering. Hand-picked zippers, loops and buttons, and hidden closures with buttons or snaps are some of the possibilities.

An imaginative closure with eye-catching buttons can transform a garment, so give plenty of thought to both technical and aesthetic considerations. When choosing buttons, or any sort of closure, evaluate proportion and ease of use. It's no fun struggling with buttons that are too large or too heavy every time you open or close a garment; and they will, over time, create strain.

Consider the weight of the closure. Are the "perfect" buttons simply too heavy, dragging the garment downward? Will a zipper, even if flexible, disturb the flow of the garment? Is it a better idea to use a number of lightweight buttons or even a hidden placket with snaps?

When applying a closure that will span two garment sections (a bodice and a skirt, for example), remember to check that the openings are exactly the same length. Does the waistline fall at precisely the same spot on both sides of the opening? Are both sides of the skirt opening exactly the same length? Are both sides of the bodice opening exactly the same length? Now, before the closure is applied, is the time to make any adjustments, which, at this point, are easy to do.

Machine-stitched zippers

Before you begin, it's worth searching for a fully adjustable zipper foot. It will give you the ability to make minute adjustments in placement, rather than relying on just a few (usually too few) preset zipper-foot positions.

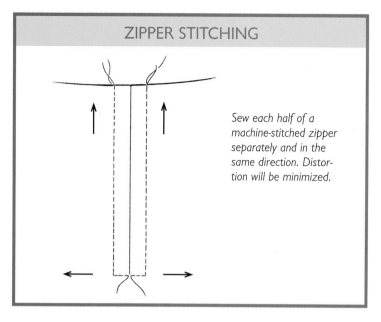

Sew each half of a machine-stitched zipper separately and in the same direction. Distortion will be minimized.

GROSGRAIN UNDERLAY

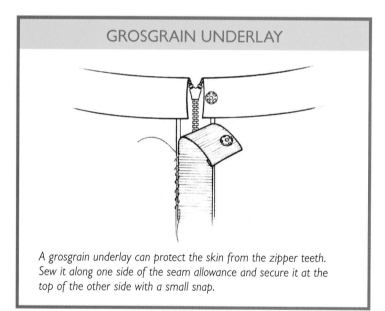

A grosgrain underlay can protect the skin from the zipper teeth. Sew it along one side of the seam allowance and secure it at the top of the other side with a small snap.

easier to get in and out of the garment. Be sure a longer opening is attractive, though, and doesn't look strangely long.

Exposed and separating zippers can make a statement, although decorative plastic and metal separating zippers may be too heavy for all but the sturdiest cottons and linens, and even then, they must be used with adequate inner support. Be sure the zipper teeth won't show (unless you want them to), especially if the garment is tight fitting.

Place a row of staystitching on either side of the zipper opening, just inside the seamline. For more strength, consider fusing interfacing to the seam allowances. Check carefully to make sure that your interfacing doesn't restrict the fabric's natural movement, especially if the zipper is on a curved seam (a side-zipper installation on a skirt, for example). Narrow strips of silk organza, butted against the fold lines of the zipper placket, are often enough to strengthen the zipper area. They are held in place when the zipper is stitched. Machine-stitch slowly to guarantee well-placed, even stitches.

On a centered application, stitch both sides in the same direction—from the bottom to the top (see the top drawing at left). Matching will be easier, and minute adjustments to accommodate any shifting that may have taken place during stitching can be made at the top edge. In tight garments without an underlay or placket (where skin might get caught in the zipper), you can easily and quickly create one by stitching a piece of grosgrain ribbon to one side of the zipper's seam allowance (see the bottom drawing at left). Use a snap to hold the grosgrain in place at the top of the zipper.

Hand-picked zippers

No other zipper installation matches the control possible with a hand-picked zipper. It is sewn carefully, stitch by stitch, its placement guided and manipulated with

Here is some basic information for machine-stitched zippers (centered, lapped, and invisible) that will help you achieve successful results. Be sure to preshrink zippers, both regular and invisible. Consider making the zippers on skirts and trousers longer than the standard 7 in. It will be

your hands. The control you have in placing stripes, plaids, and textures is unmatched by any other kind of zipper insertion. And it's surprisingly sturdy, as well as attractive and easy to do. It's a natural choice for looser weaves, where the tiny backstitches (prick stitches) practically disappear.

To install a hand-picked zipper, use double thread coated with beeswax. The zipper is sewn on with a variation of the backstitch. The stitches become so small that little thread is visible on the surface, just enough to form the stitch. Don't pull the stitches too tight, or they will disappear into the fabric and keep it from being smooth. If they are pulled extremely tight, they'll pucker the surface. The strength is in the thread, not in how tightly the stitches are pulled. The stitches should only be tight enough to rest gently on the surface of the fabric.

Start stitching at the top of one side of the open placket, working down to the bottom, then up from the bottom to the top of the other side (see the drawing at right). Your thread probably won't be long enough to do both sides, so it's better to start afresh at the beginning of the second side than to have to rethread mid-row. Also, you needn't stitch across the bottom of the zipper. Your stitches will extend slightly below the placket opening, giving you all the security you need. If you were to stitch across the bottom, it would be all too easy to pull the thread too tight and create a pucker. Try to match the placement of the stitches on the second side with those on the first side.

Once the zipper has been sewn in, there may be minute adjustments at the top of the placket to redraw the waistline or neckline. Be sure to make them before treating the top of the zipper area further.

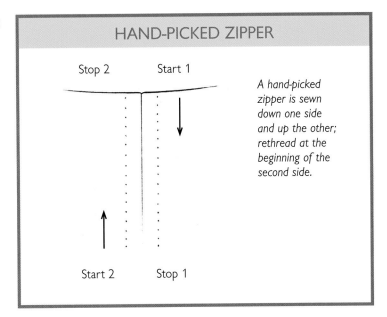

HAND-PICKED ZIPPER

Stop 2   Start 1

Start 2   Stop 1

A hand-picked zipper is sewn down one side and up the other; rethread at the beginning of the second side.

Buttons

Cottons and linens can't support terribly heavy buttons unless the garment is adequately reinforced from within, and they might look out of place. And unless you plan to remove and then resew them every time your garment is washed or dry-cleaned, be sure that the buttons you choose are compatible with the garment's cleaning requirements.

Don't choose buttons with a shank if they are decorative (unless they are secured into a nonfunctioning bound buttonhole, for example). They won't be sufficiently supported and will droop and distort the garment, and they won't match the look of the buttons that really do button. If they're heavy, reinforcing buttons at the back may help distribute their weight, but be sure they aren't visible from the right side of the garment.

Sometimes the area to which the button is sewn needs to be interfaced, especially if the fabric is at all loosely woven. Sew the buttons on with beeswax-coated thread (iron it first to encourage the beeswax to penetrate the fibers), matching the position of all the buttons and the way they're stitched on. If they'll button through any sort of thickness, you'll need to create a shank, using pins or wooden matches or even toothpicks to help you lift the thread above the button as you sew. Tailor the length of the shank accordingly.

On a shirt, avoid placing a button at the waistline if the shirt will be tucked in. On a skirt or trousers, avoid placing a button at the waistline if it will be worn with a belt. Try to eliminate a buttonhole in a waistband. There are usually too many layers of fabric to sew through successfully. A sturdy pair of hooks and eyes with a snap to hold an underlap in place is a better choice. A decorative nonfunctioning button can always be sewn at the waistband.

Machine-made buttonholes

Machine-made buttonholes on cotton and linen require nothing special technically, apart from a little inner stabilization if the fabric seems to require it. Although there are formulas for determining buttonhole length, calculated by the size of the button, you'll still need to experiment to find the correct thread, stitch width and density, and interfacing.

You may prefer to use a decorative thread, and you may decide to respace or regroup the placement of the buttons and buttonholes. A lightweight cotton may benefit from a greater number of smaller buttons, and the buttons may look more attractive grouped in pairs or trios.

If you decide to use buttons larger or smaller than those recommended by the pattern, be sure to adjust the buttonhole length, and even the width of the button stand (the area between the button line—which is usually, but not always, the center front) and the closing edge.

Buttonholes usually start $\frac{1}{8}$ in. from the button line, in the direction of the closing edge, to allow for the shank. The stand must be at least the width of the button, and for larger buttons, the width of the button plus $\frac{1}{2}$ in. Buttonholes at the top of the button line are placed at least half the button width plus $\frac{1}{4}$ in. from the top edge. They are seldom placed closer than 3 in. to 4 in. from the bottom edge, and almost never through the hem.

Use thread basting to mark the placement for the buttonholes. I don't use marking tape because it might leave a residue on the fabric, and, if stitched through, it will gum up the needle and thread.

Interfacing may be a good idea. Choose an interfacing that doesn't have any stretch on the grain that is parallel to the buttonhole lips. You may decide to reinforce the entire area or just the area around the buttonhole. If you interface just the buttonhole area, be sure that the presence of the fusible isn't detectable from the right side. Its outer edges may be visible, or it may have an effect on the fabric's texture. If it is visible, try pinking its edges to soften them or consider using instead silk organza, its grain matching that of the fashion fabric.

Before stitching the buttonholes, trim out the seam allowances, especially those near the neckline; you don't want the seam allowances caught up in the stitching. Also, they are likely to throw off your buttonhole attachment and disrupt the stitching.

If you're unhappy with the stitching, cut it away (before cutting the buttonhole) carefully and slowly, and redo it. Press the fabric before you try again, though, as it may have become distorted.

After the buttonholes are stitched and cut, you can use a little fray retardant to seal their ends, but use it carefully, making sure it doesn't seep through onto the fashion

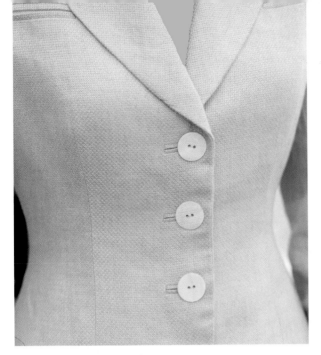

Although the fabric is somewhat loosely woven, it's been interfaced with a fusible, rendering it stable enough for bound buttonholes.

Bias self-fabric loops are an attractive alternative to machine-sewn buttonholes.

fabric. Use an indelible marker to color in any show-through from the inner layers of interfacing and/or underlining.

Bound buttonholes

Bound buttonholes can look stunning on cotton and linen garments (see the photo at left above). The clean lines and sharp edges suit these fabrics beautifully. Just be sure the fabric isn't too loosely woven for them to work well.

If the fabric isn't up to the demands of bound buttonholes, consider making non-functioning bound buttonholes, with hidden fabric-covered snaps doing the actual work. But bear in mind that this treatment works only with jackets and cuffs that remain unopened. Otherwise, the deception would be revealed.

As always, experiment. A good fusible, well applied, will give the stability you need. It will not only keep the fabric from fraying, but also will help support the strain on the buttonhole area or the welt pocket area. You'll probably want to reinforce the welts, or lips, as well, for stability. When formed with cotton or linen, they are seldom corded; that would add too much bulk.

It's easy to maintain consistency of length, width, and placement when making bound buttonholes on clearly textured cottons and linens. It's almost like sewing on graph paper.

Loops

Loops are an attractive and easy-to-create alternative to buttonholes (see the photo at right above). If your fashion fabric isn't tightly woven enough to form sturdy loops, it's the perfect opportunity to incorporate another fabric of a different color and even texture. Loops also look as good on the back side as they do on the front.

If you're replacing buttonholes with loops, a separate facing will be needed to cover their raw ends. If the garment is lined, the

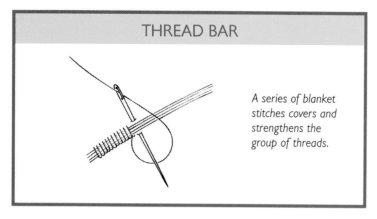

THREAD BAR

A series of blanket stitches covers and strengthens the group of threads.

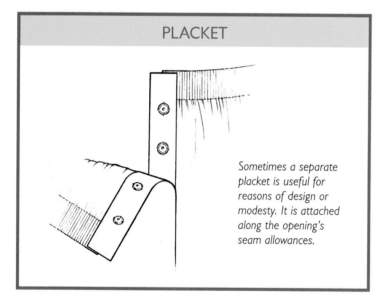

PLACKET

Sometimes a separate placket is useful for reasons of design or modesty. It is attached along the opening's seam allowances.

the bias a little as you go. Remember that after they've been turned, you'll be stretching them more, and they'll be narrower once stretched.

After you've stitched the loops and trimmed the desired amount off the seam allowance, turn them right side out. Dampen the loops, and pin them to your ironing board to get the stretch out (you don't want them to stretch once they're on the garment), making sure the seamline is straight. Wait until they're dry to unpin them. I like to pin the loops a second time, after they've been cut into the lengths I need. I shape them as they'll be shaped on the garment, making sure that the seam is along the inside of each curve.

Next, mark the placement of the loops with a row of staystitching or basting. It is important they be carbon copies of one another, perfectly spaced and angled. Be sure to baste them securely in place before machine-stitching, or the weight of the presser foot will misalign them.

Hooks and eyes

Hooks and eyes are easy enough to install (they will be stronger if sewn on with waxed double thread and more attractive if stitched on with a blanket stitch). In instances where the presence of a metal bar is jarring, consider making fabric eyes with a thread bar. Using waxed thread, go back and forth several times to create the bar, then strengthen it by covering the threads with blanket or buttonhole stitches (see the top drawing at left). Thread bars are attractive and strong; just be sure to make them the right length. If they are too long, the hooks will slip out.

Plackets

Sometimes a separate placket needs to be created at an opening. It can be formed by widening the seam allowances, but it often benefits from the reinforcement of separate

lining can double as the facing, coming right up to the looped edge.

Loops are always made on the bias, as they have to curve. Be sure that your bias is absolutely true, both when you cut it and when you stitch it. Otherwise, even though the loops are usually small, drag lines will form, and the loops won't shape the way you want them to.

Experiment with the width and roundness of the loops. The more seam allowance left in the loops, the fatter the loops will be. Use a small stitch to sew them, stretching

pieces of fabric. Plackets often close with snaps (see the bottom drawing on the facing page); for this reason they usually aren't used in areas where there is a great deal of strain. They work well with full skirts, where a zipper might interrupt the loft of the garment. A lightweight snapped placket nestles unobtrusively in the fullness of the skirt.

Darted zipper openings

Full skirts often have a center back seam to accommodate a zipper. One way to avoid this seam is to create a darted zipper opening. Instead of a seam, a vertical cut is made in the fabric. Rather than facing the opening with a separate piece of fabric, its raw edges are turned back, and near its base, the opening is melded into a dart (see the drawing and photo at right). Darted openings work well on circular skirts, where a center back seam would interrupt the flow of the skirt. The seam might pucker, contrasting with the bias and near-bias hang of the surrounding fabric. The slash, which is cut on the straight of grain, is a few inches longer than the zipper.

The dart begins at the base of the zipper and goes down into the body of the skirt for a few inches. The folds of the skirt usually camouflage its presence. Simply fold the fabric along the proposed opening and press along the fold. You can either stitch the dart and then cut the opening or make the opening and then stitch the dart—it really doesn't matter. Once the dart is sewn and the opening has been made, press back the seam allowances of the opening and press the dart open as far as you can. The raw edges will need to be finished before the zipper is inserted. You can serge, zigzag, or hand-overcast the edges. All these methods work well. Interfacing is rarely necessary, as the opening is on the straight of grain. Finish by installing the zipper by hand or by machine.

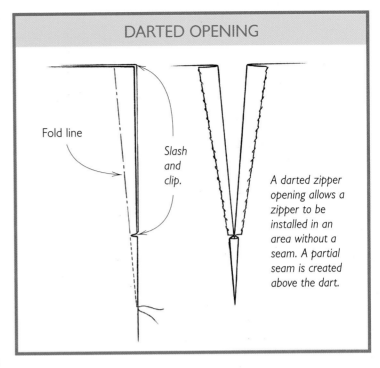

DARTED OPENING

Fold line

Slash and clip.

A darted zipper opening allows a zipper to be installed in an area without a seam. A partial seam is created above the dart.

A dart is formed below the zipper opening on this soft cotton. The raw edges have been hand-overcast.

HEMS

The purpose of a hem, regardless of where it's located, is to finish off an edge securely, in a manner compatible with the fashion fabric. Unless finished otherwise for decorative purposes, hems should be unobtrusive.

Just as a picture frame defines the perimeter of what it encloses, the hem plays a part in defining the garment's outline. Whether it's a quietly finished, barely detectable hemline, a striking scalloped edge, carefully placed rows of topstitching, or a beautifully uniform narrow hem for a lightweight circular skirt, hems are an important detail, worthy of your full attention and care.

I've always loved hemming garments. There's something tidy and straightforward about the process, especially with cotton and linen, the least finicky of fabrics to hem. They don't slip, slide, or distort. There's nothing to be concerned with from a technical point of view, other than exercising your preference for an attractive hem that's consistent in design and care with the rest of the garment.

As always, start with questions. Does the hem want to make a design statement? Is it appropriate to add design elements to the hem, such as a trim, a shaped edge, or topstitching? Will the hem need extra weight and definition from a facing or interfacing? Will a lightweight hem finish enhance the nature of a soft and flowing garment? Is there apt to be any strain on the hem? What's the best length? Is there a possibility that the hem might need to be lengthened later on? Will the garment be washed or dry-cleaned? How will the hem be pressed? Although wool and silk hems are often left without a sharp press at the bottom edge, cotton and linen hems are almost always clearly defined.

Hem skirts and trousers while wearing the shoes that will eventually be worn with them. If the garment will be worn with a belt, be sure to wear it when the garment is being hemmed.

Traditional hems

In the simplest of hems, a garment's hem allowance is turned up along the hemline and stitched. Decisions to be made include the depth of the hem, the finish for the raw edges, and the stitch that will be used. Sometimes shallow hems are simply turned twice and machine-stitched (much sportswear and many linings are hemmed this way). Be careful there's no shifting of the layers, or drag lines will form, spoiling the hem's clean look.

Deeper hems (2 in. to 2½ in. is a good depth) require a finish for the raw edge. It can be turned under, zigzagged, serged, bound with a Hong Kong finish, or trimmed with lace hem tape.

Lightweight cotton and linen sometimes benefit from a turned and stitched hem that is hand-finished with a slipstitch (see the drawing on the facing page). This treatment works well on a deep hem (one without shaping; that is, a full, gathered skirt shaped from a rectangle, for example). Simply turn the raw edge in, then turn up the hem allowance along the hemline, and slipstitch it in place. The slipstitches will be hidden in the fold of the hem allowance, with only tiny dots of thread showing on the right side of the garment. It's a clean hem treatment, and the depth of the hem allowance adds a little bit of weight and swing along the bottom of the skirt.

On some hems, one in sheer handkerchief linen for example, the first turnback can equal the depth of the hem allowance. The difference in color created by the three layers of fabric almost gives the appearance of a horizontal pleat along the hem. It can be a striking detail, echoing, perhaps, a design element featured elsewhere on the garment.

On circular skirts, where the raw edge is larger in circumference than the finished edge, hem lace allows excess fullness to be pulled in by stretching the hem lace as it's stitched on. Once the hem lace relaxes, the fashion fabric will be pulled in as the hem lace retracts. Be careful, though, not to stretch the hem lace too much.

The more flare a skirt has, the shallower the hem can be, with less fabric to ease. On a flared skirt, you can reduce the hem depth to 1½ in., or even 1 in.

Hems can be interfaced; the sturdiest result will be attained by interfacing the hem and the hem allowance. For the lightest effect, interface the hem allowance only. Interfacing on the bias will create a softly curving hem. It also adds depth and definition to a topstitched hem.

The hem can be stitched with a catchstitch or an invisible hemstitch. Hide stitches inside the edge treatment to lessen the possibility of catching them on something—the heel of a shoe, for example. Knot or backstitch the thread every 5 in. or 6 in.—that way, if the hem gets snagged, all will not be lost. Pick up as little fashion fabric as possible—only a thread or two. Remember, you're not trying to support a huge amount of weight. You're only keeping a relatively small strip of fabric in place.

If you've underlined, the stitches can go onto the underlining instead of the fashion fabric. The underlining will also give definition to the hemline.

Narrow machine hem

A narrow machine-stitched hem is an ideal way to hem a circular (or similarly full) skirt. A wide hem allowance can be troublesome on a circular skirt—much easing is required, and it's difficult to distribute the excess fabric evenly. A narrow machine hem easily absorbs the small difference in

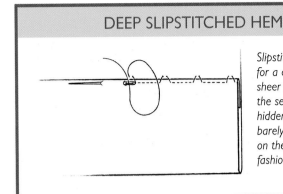

DEEP SLIPSTITCHED HEM

Slipstitching is ideal for a deep, straight, sheer hem because the sewing is virtually hidden, apart from barely visible stitches on the outside of the fashion fabric.

circumference between the raw edge and the hemline. It's also a relatively quick finish, an important consideration, given that the circumference of a circular skirt can be as great as 8 yd. A narrow hand-stitched hem, no matter how carefully applied, won't have the consistency and definition of a carefully stitched narrow machine hem. Although this treatment incorporates three rows of stitching only, two rows will be visible from the inside, and only a single row will be visible from the outside. The drawing on p. 132 summarizes the process.

A circular skirt, much of which is on varying degrees of the bias, needs to be allowed to hang. The inner tension of the threads is released when the fabric is cut, and they need time (at least 24 hours), weight, and gravity to reestablish their placement. The length can then be adjusted—either from the hemline or the waist. Keep in mind that a full-cut bias skirt will fall differently if the waist is adjusted. If the skirt is pulled up at the waist, the flare of the skirt at the center front will increase. Be aware of this effect; you may or may not want it, or it may be so minimal that it isn't a concern.

I always like to iron a bias skirt before marking the hem, just in case there's any last-minute stretching or shifting. If applying a narrow machine hem, first check that there is enough thread in your top spool

1. Staystitching

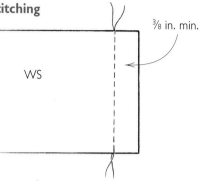

⅜ in. min.

WS

Allowing at least a ⅜-in. seam allowance (anything less is difficult to manipulate) and stitching on the wrong side of the fabric, sew a line of staystitching just below the intended hemline.

2. Pressing

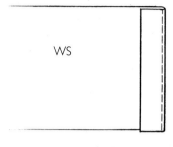

WS

Fold and press along the just sewn row of staystitches, favoring the stitches so they fall just inside the fold line.

3. Second row of stitching

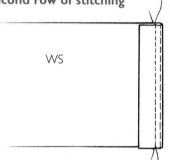

WS

Sew a second row of stitches just to the left of, and parallel to, the first row of stitching.

4. Trimming

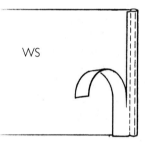

WS

Carefully trim away the seam allowance close to the second row of stitching.

5. Pressing

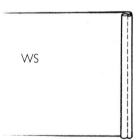

WS

Fold over along the trimmed edge and press the seam allowance; the first row of stitching is no longer visible.

6. Third row of stitching

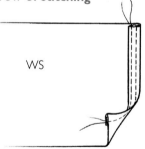

WS

RS

Place a third and final row of stitching to the left of the second row. This is the only row of stitching that will be visible from the right side of the garment.

and bobbin—it's tiresome to have to camouflage the thread join on such a carefully worked hem. Take care that your tension is as it should be and that the stitching is absolutely consistent. Work all rows of stitching (there will be three) in the same direction, with the inside of the garment facing up as you stitch. Place a row of staystitching ¼ in. to ³⁄₁₆ in. below the hemline, and at least ⅜ in. from the raw edge (Step 1 in the drawing). Any less of a seam allowance will be difficult to work with. Don't pull as you stitch, or the edge will distort. Check the hem placement carefully. A number of rows of stitching will go onto the fabric, and later alteration will be difficult and tedious.

This first row of stitching is the most important—it establishes the hemline and acts as staystitching. It also allows you to assess the placement of the hem. It's easy to spot and correct any adjustments that are needed at this point. Fold and press along the stitching line (Step 2), favoring the stitches toward the raw edge. This will keep them out of sight later.

Now sew a second row of stitching along the fold line, just to the left of the previous row of stitching (Step 3). Trim away the excess fabric close to the second row of stitching (Step 4). Work carefully with either appliqué scissors or embroidery scissors. It's a tedious task, but be patient, for the slightest inattention can lead to cutting the fashion fabric in the wrong place. There is little room for error.

Press the narrow edge up approximately ⅛ in. (Step 5), and sew a third and final row of stitching just to the left of the second row of stitches (Step 6). When you get to the end of the final row of stitching, bring the ends of the threads to the inside, knot and clip rather than overlapping them on the outside. There's no need to use pins at any point in the process. Careful pressing and guiding with your hands will give you all the control you need.

These scallops echo the shaping of the lace; they are made sturdy by a facing that doubles the entire skirt.

Faced hems

Sometimes hems need to be faced because there isn't enough fabric to form an adequate hem allowance. Other reasons to face a hem include adding definition to curves, eliminating hem stitches (if the facing goes all the way up to the waistline on a skirt, for example), backing decorative shapings such as scallops that would be difficult to hem in an ordinary manner (see the photo above), and allowing certain decorative treatments (such as piping) to be incorporated.

The facing's role in a skirt hem can be broadened to assume that of the lining, as it can elsewhere on a garment. Self-fabric forms the most compatible facing, identical in all the important ways (behavior, weight, care, reaction to pressing and moisture). When the facing extends all the way to the waist, matching darts should be pressed in opposite directions. The top edges must be aligned carefully because minute shifting and stretching are not uncommon.

Hem facings can be cut on the bias, their circumference slightly smaller than the area they're facing. No other facing duplicates the curve of a bias facing.

Straight-of-grain self-fabric bands trim the sleeves and hem of this blouse, adding style and weight.

of grain (which on a bias strip, is on the diagonal), and it can be difficult to calculate the final circumference before the band is in place, but difficult to manipulate the join once the band has been sewn in place.

I usually baste the bias in place, join the ends as accurately as possible with a machine basting stitch, stitch the band in place, and then make any necessary (usually small) adjustments to the band's circumference.

Bands are not always cut on the bias. Try to cut the band along the same grain (lengthwise or crosswise) as the garment section to which it will be attached. Fabrics are not always woven with the same number of threads per inch in their lengthwise and crosswise grains. Mixing them often results in distortion. It's a minor point, but they will have different degrees of stretch, and it may be detectable.

If you're hand-stitching the inside edge of the band, be sure that your stitches aren't visible. They must be firm enough to hold the seam allowance in place without gaping, but loose enough not to cause any puckering. It takes experimentation to find just the right stitch (try a fell stitch or a slipstitch), stitch length, and tension.

BRA CARRIERS

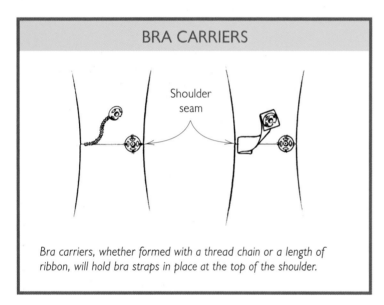

BRA CARRIERS

Shoulder seam

Bra carriers, whether formed with a thread chain or a length of ribbon, will hold bra straps in place at the top of the shoulder.

Bands

Fabric strips, or bands, are sometimes used to finish edges (see the photo above). They function primarily as a design detail, but they can also be called into play to lengthen edges that are too short. Bands cut on the bias have the advantage of being able to be shaped and of curving beautifully without forming any sharp edges, but they can be tricky to construct. They can stretch, making it difficult to maintain a constant width, and they can be hard to piece accurately. They must be pieced on the straight

Cotton and linen garments can reveal a lot of bare skin, especially around the neck and shoulder area, and the clean lines of a garment shouldn't be spoiled by the presence of visible bra straps. The straps are easily contained if held in place with bra carriers—narrow strips of ribbon or crocheted thread that snap to the garment (see the drawing at left). Bra carriers are usually placed at the top of the shoulder, anchored to the seam allowance or the lining. In certain cases, a second set can be added (farther down the back, for example, on especially narrow shoulder straps). Be careful, though, that they don't create any pulling or distortion.

THREAD CHAINS

In addition to forming bra carriers, hand-crocheted thread chains have other uses. They can be used to hold linings in place (at the hems of trousers, for example, if the lining and the trousers are independent of one another), they can hold the ends of shoulder pads in place along the armscye, and they can be used for belt carriers. Although not particularly strong, they are simple to make (see the top drawing at at right) and are sturdy enough to hold layers in place inconspicuously. Their length can easily be tailored to suit.

Be sure to anchor both ends of the thread chain in multiple layers of fabric—it will be less likely to pull through. If it does, the chain will have to be remade, and the fabric is likely to have been damaged when the chain pulled loose.

THREAD BARS

A thread bar (see the bottom drawing at right) is a series of threads covered with a row of blanket stitches. Although it's the rows of thread that do the work, it's the blanket stitches that hold the rows of thread together and allow them to work as one. A thread bar forms a strong, reasonably inconspicuous loop, and even if it is visible, it's attractive if carefully formed. Thread bars used with a metal hook and placed between the buttons of a jacket can prevent gaping. They can also form button loops at the back closure of a blouse without adding the bulk of a fabric loop. Be sure to use double thread that's coated with beeswax, and anchor the threads firmly to the fabric. If you can, use a square of reinforcing fabric, cut on the bias, at the back of the thread bar to strengthen it further.

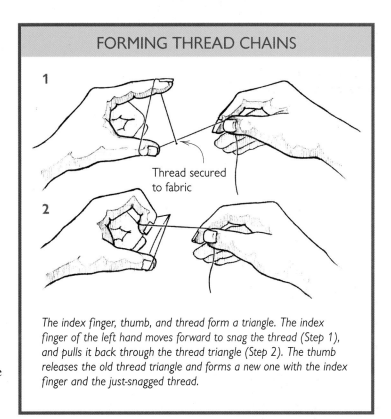

FORMING THREAD CHAINS

1

Thread secured to fabric

2

The index finger, thumb, and thread form a triangle. The index finger of the left hand moves forward to snag the thread (Step 1), and pulls it back through the thread triangle (Step 2). The thumb releases the old thread triangle and forms a new one with the index finger and the just-snagged thread.

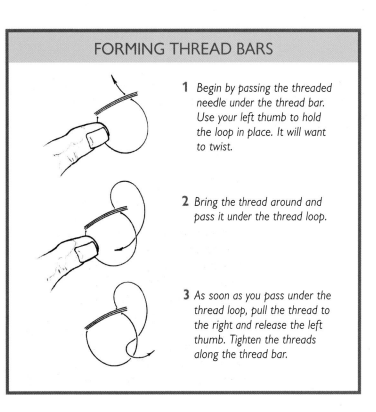

FORMING THREAD BARS

1 Begin by passing the threaded needle under the thread bar. Use your left thumb to hold the loop in place. It will want to twist.

2 Bring the thread around and pass it under the thread loop.

3 As soon as you pass under the thread loop, pull the thread to the right and release the left thumb. Tighten the threads along the thread bar.

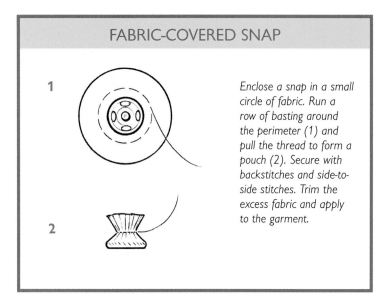

FABRIC-COVERED SNAP

1

2

Enclose a snap in a small circle of fabric. Run a row of basting around the perimeter (1) and pull the thread to form a pouch (2). Secure with backstitches and side-to-side stitches. Trim the excess fabric and apply to the garment.

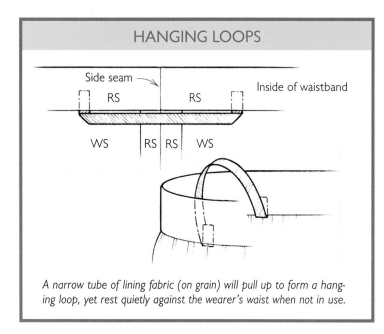

HANGING LOOPS

Side seam —

RS   RS   Inside of waistband

WS   RS RS   WS

A narrow tube of lining fabric (on grain) will pull up to form a hanging loop, yet rest quietly against the wearer's waist when not in use.

COVERED SNAPS

There are times when the presence of snaps is jarring, particularly if they're large, but snaps are easily covered, meshing style with function. Starting with a long piece of thread, hand-stitch around the edge of a circle of fabric. (The fabric you use should be tightly woven, or such a small piece will fall apart.) Put the socket half of the snap inside (socket side down) and pull the thread taut, enclosing the snap in a little pouch of fabric (see the top drawing at left). Backstitch around the perimeter, finishing with a few stitches from side to side. Trim the excess fabric that's been gathered in the middle and flatten the remaining fabric as much as you can with your fingers. Double the remaining thread, coat it with beeswax, and sew the snap with a blanket stitch.

When working with the socket end, there's no need to make a hole for the ball; the first time the snap is used, one will usually form automatically. If the fabric is particularly tightly woven and the ball doesn't want to go into the socket, make a tiny hole with the tip of your scissors. The ball will open it further when the two pieces are snapped. To cover the ball end of the snap, make a tiny slit in the center of the fabric circle, slip the ball through, and proceed as before.

BLANKET-STITCHED CLOSURES

Many closures are decorative, or if they're not, they're hidden. Sometimes, though, it's difficult to camouflage hooks and eyes and snaps. If they're not too tiny, snaps can be covered with fabric, as explained above, and thread bars can replace metal eyes (see p. 135). When these details can't be hidden, you can add a little bit of style by sewing them on with a neatly applied blanket stitch (see the photo on the facing page). Use double thread coated with beeswax— it will be sturdier as well as easier to stitch.

HANGING LOOPS

Cotton and linen garments are seldom weighty enough to present difficulties while being hung, but you will want to keep your garments as free of distortion and wrinkles as possible. Here's a variation on traditional hanging loops for skirts and trousers that's easy to install, flat, and invisible and has the added advantage of distributing the garment's weight from four points instead of two. Using a narrow tube of on-grain fashion fabric (if it's fairly light in weight) or the lining, insert it into the base of the waistband, on the inside of the garment (see the bottom drawing on the facing page). Sew one end a few inches to the left of the side seam and the other a few inches to the right of the seam. Match its position and length at the opposite side of the waistband. When the garment is being worn, the loops will curve and lie flat against the wearer's waist, yet they'll pull up to form hanging loops when the garment needs to be hung.

Sleeveless dresses and tops with narrow shoulders often need hanging loops, but on such garments loops can be difficult to hide. Instead, sew the eye part of the hook-and-eye set to the inside of the shoulder seam, and the matching hook to its own padded hanger (see the top drawing at right). The wearer won't be aware of the tiny metal eye, and the garment will be held in its proper position while being stored.

DRESS SHIELDS

Don't overlook dress shields. Cotton and linen are fabrics for hot climates, and visible perspiration marks are to be avoided. They will not only spoil the appearance of a garment but in time will also stain and weaken the underarm area.

You can buy dress shields, or you can make your own (see the bottom drawing at right). Cut them from lightweight cotton, echoing the shape of the garment's underarm area, and line them with flannel to absorb perspiration. Tack the shields in place so that two-thirds of the shield is forward from the side seam. Dress shields must be removed before dry cleaning.

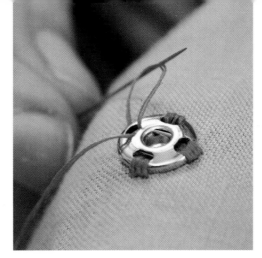

Catching the thread with the needle before pulling it taut will form a neat blanket stitch.

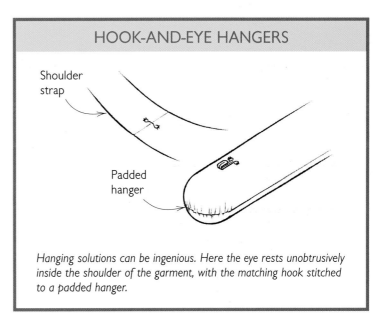

HOOK-AND-EYE HANGERS

Shoulder strap

Padded hanger

Hanging solutions can be ingenious. Here the eye rests unobtrusively inside the shoulder of the garment, with the matching hook stitched to a padded hanger.

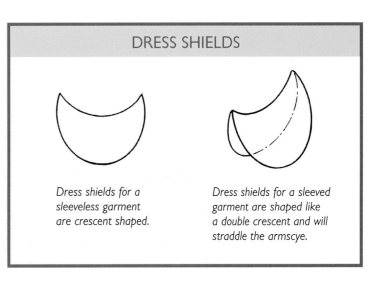

DRESS SHIELDS

Dress shields for a sleeveless garment are crescent shaped.

Dress shields for a sleeved garment are shaped like a double crescent and will straddle the armscye.

Index

Publisher: *Jim Childs*

Acquisitions Editor: *Jolynn Gower*

Editorial Assistant: *Sarah Coe*

Editors: *Ruth Dobsevage, Peter Chapman, Candace Levy*

Designer/Layout Artist: *Susan Fazekas*

Photographers: *Jack Deutsch (fashion shots), Scott Phillips (process shots)*

Illustrator: *Heather Lambert*

Indexer: *Nancy Bloomer*